# Visualizing Streaming Data
## *Interactive Analysis Beyond Static Limits*

*Anthony Aragues*

Beijing · Boston · Farnham · Sebastopol · Tokyo

**Visualizing Streaming Data**

by Anthony Aragues

Printed in Canada.

Published by O'Reilly Media, Inc., 1005 Gravenstein Highway North, Sebastopol, CA 95472.

O'Reilly books may be purchased for educational, business, or sales promotional use. Online editions are also available for most titles (*http://oreilly.com/safari*). For more information, contact our corporate/institutional sales department: 800-998-9938 or *corporate@oreilly.com*.

| | |
|---|---|
| **Acquisitions Editor:** Rachel Roumeliotis | **Indexer:** WordCo, Inc. |
| **Development Editor:** Angela Rufino | **Interior Designer:** David Futato |
| **Production Editor:** Justin Billing | **Cover Designer:** Karen Montgomery |
| **Copyeditor:** Rachel Head | **Illustrator:** Rebecca Demarest |
| **Proofreader:** Sharon Wilkey | |

June 2018:  First Edition

**Revision History for the First Edition**
2018-05-30:  First Release

See *http://oreilly.com/catalog/errata.csp?isbn=9781492031857* for release details.

978-1-492-03185-7

[TI]

# Table of Contents

# Preface

Several things converged to lead me to write this book. I'm a huge science-fiction nerd. I fell in love with fantasy user interfaces—the interfaces in movies and TV shows, often used as plot devices. When they are well done, they fit the needs of the actors perfectly—at a glance immediately conveying a status, a transition, and then a new status. I looked for years for kits to help me make real interfaces that were more like these. As I got better at programming, I realized that it always makes sense to specifically design an interface for an aesthetic and a plot instead of relying on a general working toolkit that is themed. I resigned myself to the fact that the kit I was looking for wouldn't be forthcoming.

As I broke down fantasy user interfaces into common components and logic, I realized they weren't that complex, and lots of the components would be universally useful. These fantasy UIs did break a lot of rules, though. In order to show transitions in a plot, they show things changing. Data streams in and impacts the status. Entire sections move or transform in ways we typically would not do in a dashboard. The conventional wisdom on dashboards by people like Stephen Few (*http://www.stephen-few.com/*) is that they should convey status at a glance. That can be difficult to do when everything is moving and transforming simultaneously. There is real value outside the defined conventional wisdom on what to do for dashboards; it just fits a different need. If we quit comparing our interfaces to a dashboard that already has a set purpose, we can set new rules.

A recent example can be seen in the fantasy world of Westworld on HBO (see Figure P-1). They have mock user interfaces that represent the future of technology and show current information compared to thresholds and norms. It looks amazing and is inspiring as a goal to reach in working systems.

*Figure P-1. A fantasy user interface from the show Westworld on HBO (source: http://www.vanschneider.com/behind-the-scenes-of-the-westworld-ui)*

I have been working in technology for most of my life. I have seen a lot of problems solved by looking at raw data streaming by, but in the last 20+ years I haven't really seen this evolving. Logs, events, or messages are streamed in a console, and at most they are filtered and highlighted inline. You have to be looking at the screen at the moment something displays, and if you miss it, maybe it will show up in your daily reports tomorrow. This was OK for systems that might have a line in the console per minute, but it doesn't work for today's systems, where thousands per second are typical. Even at this volume, I've seen problems solved by glancing at streaming logs that would not be caught in daily reports, where the information is too abstracted and aggregated. After observing this pattern over the years, I want to make a viable solution that falls between the logs on the console and the at-a-glance dashboard.

Technology doesn't advance itself. What I really want is to be more interactive with systems. I want things like augmented reality to be practical, unobtrusive, and helpful. When I think of what that requires, I keep seeing things that are in the way, stepping stones that must be crossed before getting there. One of the major stepping stones technology seems to be skipping over is providing an understanding of what a system decides. When artificial intelligence is deciding something for me, I want to know why. The more times I look into why something was decided and can correct those assumptions, the more trust I have in a system. Netflix does a decent job of recommending shows, and it tells you why it recommends something and what the confidence level is, but you can't correct the algorithm. It's not interactive. It observes, does magic, and you see the results.

In order for us to progress beyond a certain point in technology, we are going to have to take a couple of steps back and correct this. We have to redesign some things to allow humans to be more collaborative partners in these decisions. This is difficult today because most systems decide things for you centrally. An algorithm is applied universally. If genre and language are the key factors in recommending similar movies, that's how it's done for everyone. There's nowhere that I know of where I can increase the weight of awesome fantasy user interfaces and novel spaceship design to find movies that might interest me. This level of customization requires the intelligence to be more individual, or multitiered.

The significance of being able to understand and alter machine decisions goes way beyond entertainment. AI algorithms thoroughly influence your perspective through the information you see—they determine the results of your Internet searches. When you access information online, security devices decide what information appears safe (with a very loose yet inflexible definition of "safe"). On the physical side of security, we have algorithms deciding who is on a watchlist and who might commit crimes. Similarly complex algorithms have not been permitted in the assessment of credit scores because they must be easily defensible in court. That's the level of accountability and understanding all automated decisions need to reach.

Finally, I started developing my own tools and components to fit this niche area of data presentation I kept running across. After years of thought on the subject, I realized that it was something rarely explored. Most of the organizations I run into are overwhelmed by what they find in their daily reports. They aren't thinking about what they might improve by reacting faster to certain events and getting ahead of things. It takes some new perspectives, case studies, and more to take something like this from a novel idea to a practical solution. I hope that this book helps contribute toward that progression.

# Who This Book Will Benefit

If you are a designer or developer who has any event-based data significant to your goals, you will find something of interest here. The topics ride the line between design and development because they are both integral in presenting comprehensible data.

If you are already trying to watch data by scrolling it in a console, or you've given up on scrolling data in the console because it wasn't helping, this book will give you some approaches to explore.

If you are interested in creating a system for your needs that exposes what's occurring in an opaque process, this book will give you an idea of what you can do to improve your system's visibility.

## How This Book Is Organized

This book is organized from the perspective of "how to build it." There are a lot of possible starting points. If you already have streaming data in a format ready to be shown, you might skip ahead to the chapters on presentation. Many organizations still haven't reached this point. They have data that is event-based by nature but no good way to connect to it. This book walks through those points as well, and everything in between. Some topics, like machine learning, are simply complementary and optional. Figure P-2 represents a logical progression of components and processes that are involved in visualizing streaming data to integrated analysts with automated processing in a complex system. This workflow is the the oultine for the order of the chapters in this book.

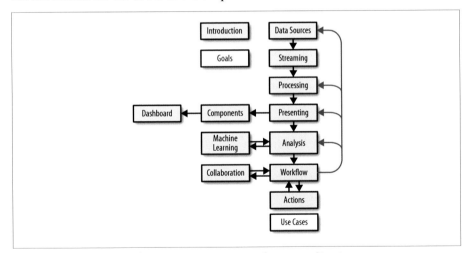

*Figure P-2. Data flow of interactive streaming data visualizations*

## Conventions Used in This Book

The following typographical conventions are used in this book:

*Italic*
    Indicates new terms, URLs, email addresses, filenames, and file extensions.

Constant width

Used for program listings, as well as within paragraphs to refer to program elements such as variable or function names, databases, data types, environment variables, statements, and keywords.

# Using Code Examples

Supplemental material (code examples, exercises, etc.) is available for download at *https://github.com/SuddenDevelopment/Visualizing-Streaming-Data*.

This book is here to help you get your job done. In general, if example code is offered with this book, you may use it in your programs and documentation. You do not need to contact us for permission unless you're reproducing a significant portion of the code. For example, writing a program that uses several chunks of code from this book does not require permission. Selling or distributing a CD-ROM of examples from O'Reilly books does require permission. Answering a question by citing this book and quoting example code does not require permission. Incorporating a significant amount of example code from this book into your product's documentation does require permission.

We appreciate, but do not require, attribution. An attribution usually includes the title, author, publisher, and ISBN. For example: "*Visualizing Streaming Data* by Anthony Aragues (O'Reilly). Copyright 2018 Anthony Aragues, 978-1-492-03185-7."

If you feel your use of code examples falls outside fair use or the permission given above, feel free to contact us at *permissions@oreilly.com*.

# O'Reilly Safari

 *Safari* (formerly Safari Books Online) is a membership-based training and reference platform for enterprise, government, educators, and individuals.

Members have access to thousands of books, training videos, Learning Paths, interactive tutorials, and curated playlists from over 250 publishers, including O'Reilly Media, Harvard Business Review, Prentice Hall Professional, Addison-Wesley Professional, Microsoft Press, Sams, Que, Peachpit Press, Adobe, Focal Press, Cisco Press, John Wiley & Sons, Syngress, Morgan Kaufmann, IBM Redbooks, Packt, Adobe Press, FT Press, Apress, Manning, New Riders, McGraw-Hill, Jones & Bartlett, and Course Technology, among others.

For more information, please visit *http://oreilly.com/safari*.

# How to Contact Us

Please address comments and questions concerning this book to the publisher:

O'Reilly Media, Inc.
1005 Gravenstein Highway North
Sebastopol, CA 95472
800-998-9938 (in the United States or Canada)
707-829-0515 (international or local)
707-829-0104 (fax)

We have a web page for this book, where we list errata, examples, and any additional information. You can access this page at *http://bit.ly/visualizing-streaming-data*.

To comment or ask technical questions about this book, send email to *bookquestions@oreilly.com*.

For more information about our books, courses, conferences, and news, see our website at *http://www.oreilly.com*.

Find us on Facebook: *http://facebook.com/oreilly*

Follow us on Twitter: *http://twitter.com/oreillymedia*

Watch us on YouTube: *http://www.youtube.com/oreillymedia*

# Acknowledgments

Bob Page (*https://www.linkedin.com/in/bobpage/*) thoughtfully reviewed everything I had on the subject in detail, lending his expertise on data in large businesses. He also introduced me to people who had a big impact on this material.

Antonio Figueiredo (*https://www.linkedin.com/in/afigueiredo/*) has a lot of real-world experience in making streaming data processing and visualization practical. His enthusiasm on the subject and general willingness to discuss everything related was a huge encouragement early on.

Sven Krasser (*https://www.linkedin.com/in/svenkrasser/*) is an old colleague and known expert in machine learning. It was through working with him that I saw the need to make people more interactive in the machine learning process.

Brett Meyer (*https://www.linkedin.com/in/brett-meyer-0ab9251b/*) helped me explore the various ways that streaming data visualization would and would not make sense when applied to machine learning. His expertise helped me find the correct terms and understand their use in that field.

Georges Grinstein (*https://www.linkedin.com/in/georgesgrinstein/*) is a well-known expert in data visualization, including real-time and streaming data. He has an academic perspective on several things that I had not previously considered and showed me some interesting and relevant projects I wouldn't have been able to find on my own.

Casey Rosenthal (*https://www.linkedin.com/in/caseyrosenthal/*) created one of the most useful and relevant case studies that I was able to learn from outside my own experience. He was helpful in sharing those experiences as well as talking about where this niche area should go.

Weidong Yang (*https://www.linkedin.com/in/yangweidong/*) basically makes a business out of the topic of this book. His company creates interactive installations that gather and present data in creative ways. He was helpful in sharing these experiences, but also helped validate that this topic has a current market.

Raffael Marty (*https://www.linkedin.com/in/raffy/*) was the unintentional catalyst for my writing this book. I took a seminar of his on security data visualization; I enjoyed it and thought I'd enjoy teaching a similar one someday.

# CHAPTER 1

# Introduction

Administrators, analysts, and developers have been watching data fly by on screens for decades. The fast, free, and most common method is to "tail" a log file. `tail` is a standard Unix-like operating system command that allows you to stream all changes to a specified file to the command line. Without any additional options, the logs will display in the console without any filtering or formatting. Despite the overwhelming amount of data scrolling past, it's still a common practice because the people watching can often catch a glimpse of something significant that is missed by other tools. When filtering and formatting are applied to this simple method, it increases the ease and likelihood of catching significant events that would otherwise be ignored or surfaced only after a significant delay. LNav is an application that represents streaming infromation on a console with some ability to highlight and filter information (see Figure 1-1).

Because of the rate at which information is scrolling by, anything noticed by a human observer with this method will be due to them observing either a pattern or the breaking of a pattern. Statistics, aggregates, groupings, comparisons, and analysis are out of reach for this method at a high data frequency. This method also has a limitation of one log file per command line. In order to progress from this standard of streaming data visualization, this book will explore ways to preserve and build on the effect of noticing something significant in live events. The challenge is how to do this without abstracting the context so far that it becomes another dashboard of statistics that sends the observer back to the tried and true method of command-line scrolling.

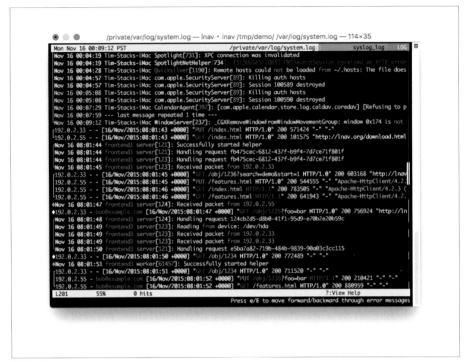

*Figure 1-1. A log file viewer (source: http://lnav.org)*

A great analogy for visualizing streaming data is visualizing operational intelligence, described in a Netflix database project (*https://github.com/Netflix/atlas/wiki*) as follows:

> Whereas business intelligence is data gathered for analyzing trends over time, operational intelligence provides a picture of what is currently happening within a system.

Operational intelligence relies heavily on streaming data. The data is usually automatically processed, and alerts are sent when anything goes outside of a defined threshold. Visualizing this information allows people to better understand what's occurring, and whether any automated decisions should be created, deleted, or adjusted.

# Why Visualizations

Visualizations certainly can be eye candy, but their value isn't just in attracting eyeballs and mesmerizing people. In general, visualizations can give you a new perspective on data that you simply wouldn't be able to get otherwise. Even at the smaller scale of individual records, a visualization can speed up your ingestion of content by giving you visual cues that you can process much faster than reading the data. Here are a few benefits of adding a visualization layer to your data:

- Improved pattern/anomaly recognition
- Higher data density, allowing you to see a much broader spectrum of data
- Visual cues to understand the data faster and quickly pick out attributes
- Summaries of the data as charted statistics
- Improved ability to conquer assumptions made about the data
- Greater context and understanding of scale, position, and relevance

On top of all that, visualizations also help products sell, get publicity, and screenshot well. Visualizations attract people and entice them to make sense of what they see. They become necessary when trying to understand more complex data such as the automated decisions behind an organization's operational intelligence.

# The Standard

The processes and applications that we accept as tried and true were written for a different set of circumstances than we are faced with today. There will continue to be a place for them for the problems they were developed to solve, but they were not designed for the volume, frequency, variance, and context that we are seeing now and that will only increase over time.

There are recent highly scalable solutions for processing and storing this data, but visualizing the data is left behind as we resign ourselves to the idea that humans can't possibly review all of it in time to have an impact. Visualizing the data is required only for *people* to understand it. As processes are developed to deal with this post-human scale, visualizations are falling by the wayside—and along with them our ability to gain immediate insights and make improvements to the applications. The same problem occurs if too many processing steps are hidden from view. Examples of this effect are the inverse of the defined goals of streaming data visualization:

- Missing a significant pattern that can be intuitively found by a person but that would be difficult to predict ahead of time and develop into an application
- Missing something anomalous that would justify an immediate action
- Seeing a security-related event as an alert and out of the surrounding context
- Seeing a threshold pass as an alert, with a limited view of what led to it
- Only preprogrammed understanding of the evolution of the data over time

# Terms

*Streaming data* is not a canonized technical term. Its meaning can vary based on environment and context. It's often interchanged with *real-time data* and *live data*. Streaming data is any data that is currently transmitting in a serial fashion as events occur. For the purposes of this book, we will also specify that the stream is at a rate of at least 10 records per second, or around 1 million records per day. This rate is too high for a single person to be able to watch the data and get anything meaningful from it without the help of some data processes and applications. This is also a conservative rate of data for modern applications and internet services. The Wikimedia network broadcasts hundreds of edits per second in a publicly available data stream.

*Visualization* is a generic term for any way to present data to a person. We will divide it into a few categories for later reference:

*Raw data*
> Shown in the original format, such as a log line

*Tabular data*
> Shown in a grid of columns and rows, so that common fields are aligned vertically and each record has its own row

*Statistics and aggregates*
> Shown as charts and dashboards of hand-picked details that have significance

*Visualizations*
> Abstract representations of data for intuitive interpretation by the analyst

All of these categories have a long history of use and well-defined use cases. They have been in use since print media was the norm and haven't advanced much, partially because the conventional wisdom has been to keep them compatible with a printable report. Being print-compatible makes it easy to get a snapshot at any time to include in a paper report, but also enforces limitations.

*Analysts* are the primary people to whom data is being displayed. They are the ones performing interactive analyses on the data presented.

# Data Formats

There are a lot of different formats that raw data can come in. We need to work with whatever format is output and transform it into the format that we need for any downstream processes, such as showing it in a visualization. The first significant attribute of a data format is whether it's human-readable. Table 1-1 shows examples of formats that are human-readable, and Table 1-2 shows examples of formats that are not.

---

*Table 1-1. Examples of human-readable data formats*

| Format | Description | Example |
|---|---|---|
| UTF-8 | Unstructured but readable text. | There was a modification to the English Wikipedia page for the Australian TV series *The Voice* from an unknown user at the IP address 82.155.238.44. |
| CSV | Data is flat (no hierarchy) and consistent. The fields are defined in the first row, and all of the following rows contain values. Fields are delimited by a character such as a comma. | Link,item,country,user,event<br>"https://en.wikipedia.org/w/index.php?diff=742259222&oldid=740584413", "The Voice (Australian TV series)","#en.wikipedia","82.155.238.44","wiki modification" |
| XML | An early, verbose, and highly versatile format standardized to have a common approach to overcome CSV's limitations. | <xml><br><link><br>https://en.wikipedia.org/w/index.php?diff=742259222&oldid=740584413<br></link><br><item><br>The Voice (Australian TV series)<br></item><br><country><br>#en.wikipedia<br></country><br><user><br>82.155.238.44<br></user><br><event><br>wiki modification<br></event><br></xml> |
| JSON | A format designed to be more succinct than XML while retaining the advantages over CSV. | {<br>"link":"https://en.wikipedia.org/w/index.php?diff=742259222&oldid=740584413",<br>"item":"The Voice (Australian TV series)",<br>"country":"#en.wikipedia",<br>"user":"82.155.238.44",<br>"event":"wiki modification"<br>} |
| Key/value pairs | A commonly used format for an arbitrary set of fields. | Link="https://en.wikipedia.org/w/index.php?diff=742259222&oldid=740584413",<br>Item="The Voice (Australian TV series)",<br>Country=#en.wikipedia",<br>User="82.155.238.44",<br>Event="wiki modification" |

*Table 1-2. Examples of data formats that are not human-readable*

| Format | Description | Example |
| --- | --- | --- |
| Binary | The conversion of anything to a 0 or 1, or on/off state. This is rarely something necessary to work with for visualizing data. | 0111101100001010001000100110110001101001011... |
| Hex | Similar to binary, but instead of base 2, it's base 16. Hexadecimal values use the characters 0–9 and a–f. | 7B0A226C696E6B223A2268747470733A2F2F656E2E77696B69 |
| Base64 | Similar to hex, but with 64 characters available. | ewoibGluayI6Imh0dHBzOi8vZW4ud2IraXBlZGlhLm9yZy93L2... |

# Data Visualization Applications

Applications that visualize data can be divided into two categories: those that are created for specific data and those that allow visualizing any data they can attach to. General-purpose data visualization applications will allow you to quickly take the data that you have and start applying it to charts. This is a great way to proto-type what useful information you can show and understand the gaps in what might be meaningful. Eventually, a design is chosen to best make decisions from, and a context-specific visualization is created in a purpose-built application.

Another distinction we will make for this book is how the visualization applica-tion handles constantly updating data. Options include the following:

- A static visualization that uses the data that is available when the visualiza-tion is created. Any new data requires a refresh.
- A real-time visualization that looks like the static one but updates itself con-stantly.
- A streaming data visualization that shows the flow of data and the impact it has on the statistics.

# Assumptions and Setup

This introductory chapter only hints at the variations of data and the processes for manipulating it. A common set of data sources and processes will be estab-lished for reference in the rest of this book so that they can be consistently built upon and compared. The data sources are available for free and are live streams (Table 1-3). These are ideal sources to test the ideas put forth in this book. They will also provide a much-needed context focus, which is essential for effectively visualizing data.

*Table 1-3. Public test data streams*

| Data | Description | Storage | Volume |
|------|-------------|---------|--------|
| Wikimedia edits | All edits to Wikimedia as a public stream of data (*https://www.mediawiki.org/wiki/API:Recent_changes_stream*) | Document store | 300/second |
| Throttled Twitter feed by PubNub | A trickle of the Twitter firehose provided as a public demo by PubNub (*http://bit.ly/2sic18Y*) | Distributed storage | 50/second |
| Bitcoin transactions | Bitcoin transactions (*https://blockchain.info/*) with information for tracking and analyzing | Database | 20/second |

You will need to establish your own standards for formats, storage, and transport so that you have a set of tools that you know work well with each other. Then, when you run into new data that you need to work with, you should transform it from the original format into your standard as early in the workflow as possible so that you can take advantage of your established toolset.

The data format for the rest of the book will be JSON. Even if you are working with another format, JSON is flexible enough to be converted to and from various formats. Its balance between flexibility, verbosity, and use within JavaScript makes it a popular choice.

Node.js will be the primary server technology referenced. Its primary advantage is that it runs on JavaScript and can share libraries with browsers. It also happens to be a great choice for streaming data solutions that are not so large that they require dozens of servers or more.

Angular.js is the main client library used in the book. Both Angular.js and React are common and appropriate choices to show event-based data in the browser.

This combination of components is often referred to as a *MEAN stack* for MongoDB, Express.js, Angular.js, and Node.js. MongoDB is a popular document store, and Express is a web server built on Node. Mongo and Express aren't as essential to the discussion of this book, though we will review storage considerations in more detail. Several other libraries will be mentioned throughout this book as needed that build on this technical stack.

The client components, when mentioned, will be browser-based. A modern browser with at least WebSockets and WebGL is assumed. What these are and why they make sense will be detailed later, but it's a good idea to check that your browser supports them before getting started. You can do this by following these links:

- *http://caniuse.com/#feat=webgl*
- *http://caniuse.com/#feat=websockets*

# CHAPTER 2

# Goals

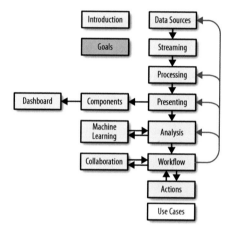

This chapter focuses on what goals will drive you in which directions for the rest of the book. Defining what you are trying to accomplish from a high level gives you a context in which to think about the rest of the information.

Given the scope of data that people are looking at, what kinds of insights are they trying to gather that justify watching a screen of data for any length of time? Possibilities include the following:

- A significant pattern that can be intuitively found by a person but that would be difficult to predict ahead of time to develop into an application
- Something anomalous that would justify an immediate action (this assumes the person has a decent understanding of the common patterns)
- Security-related events above a certain threshold of risk

- Knowing when something has passed a status threshold, or is trending toward it
- An understanding of the evolution of the data over time
- Monitoring complex, automated decisions as they occur.
- Operational intelligence insights for faster reaction time.

# Presentation Goals

Visualizations can have different goals, purposes, and intended audiences. Broadly, they fall into three categories: sales, reports, and analytics. Depending on the goal, use of streaming visualizations can be more or less effective. Table 2-1 compares the different presentation goals and considerations.

*Table 2-1. Visualization impact by audience*

|  | Known topics | Known conclusions | Q&A | Audience attention span | Audience |
|---|---|---|---|---|---|
| **Sales** | X | X | Announce the results | Instant impact | General public |
| **Reports** | X | | Answer questions | Brief consideration | Insiders |
| **Analytics** | | | Ask questions | Intense exploration | Specialists |

Visualizing data for *sales* isn't just for the purpose of making money. It comes with its own conclusion built in. It's showing the data in a way that intentionally leads or sells the user on it. When sales presentations of data are crafted, combinations of statistics and visualizations are manipulated until the message conveyed is what is intended:

> Facts are stubborn, but statistics are more pliable.
>
> —Mark Twain

Once you visualize data, you are dealing with the presentation of facts as much as the facts themselves. Statistics and visualizations are often manipulated towards a predetermined outcome in order to tell a story. I found statistics about death by food poisoning that make it sound like a huge issue. I also found similar statistics about easting disorders. None of them talks about the statistics in the same manner as the other or compared to anything else that would be relevant. Each is crafted for maximum desired impact. Data visualization has that influence as well. It is the visual equivalent to the sound byte that is easy to understand and remember.

The process to create a sales presentation is straightforward (see Figure 2-1). Data that supports an argument is collected for a static presentation. It's very deliberate and predictable.

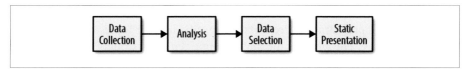

*Figure 2-1. Process for sales presentation*

The other factor in a sales visualization is the so-called "wow factor." The more eyeballs you can attract, the more people you can persuade. The more impressive-looking the presentation is, the more likely it is that people will think the conclusions presented are of equal substance. The goal of persuading an audience is a common one, and a distinct goal from other uses of visualizations.

The effectiveness of a sales visualization is based on its ability to attract attention and persuade an audience. Using streaming visualizations for a sales presentation can be difficult if the data is unpredictable. The wow factor might be there, but the conclusion an audience comes to will vary with the data they see at the time they are watching the visualization.

Figure 2-2 uses a sales presentation to achieve a more empathetic response than numbers alone. Each person is represented with their own story and profile. This presentation is effective for a message that could otherwise be lost in a broader view of the data, or one that showed deaths by other circumstances.

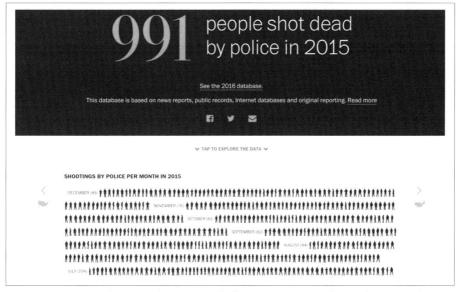

*Figure 2-2. A visualization that is intended to convey a specific predetermined conclusion (source: https://wapo.st/2Jjy1Kn)*

*Reports* contain visualizations that are intended to aid in making decisions. These can be periodic, like a report on the previous day's activity or a week in review.

They can also be dashboards that are always updated with the latest results. As opposed to sales presentations, reports are specific in their topics of focus but not their conclusions. The process for developing a report is similar to developing a sales presentation, but the answers to questions are open ended (Figure 2-3).

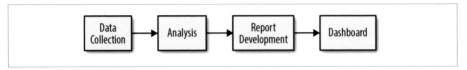

*Figure 2-3. Process for reporting presentation*

A report should use a visualization optimal for making a decision along a known path. A gauge is a good example of a common report visualization. The data for a gauge will be consistently focused on a current value. The value has a range, and there are thresholds within that range that are meaningful for a decision or conclusion. A collection of such visualizations within a theme along with supporting data will compose a report. Figure 2-4 shows examples of dashboards for business intelligence. They are developed from structured data to answer specific questions that will drive business decisions.

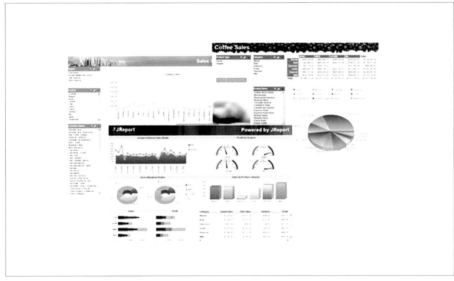

*Figure 2-4. Examples of reports for making decisions—the questions are known, but the conclusions are left to the audience (source: https://en.wikipedia.org/wiki/Dashboard_(business))*

The effectiveness of a report is based on its ability to completely, accurately, and effectively represent the information required to make the decisions necessary. Streaming data applies well to reporting dashboards. Any reporting dashboard visualization can show a stream of values to immediately add some recent context of frequency, patterns, and value consistency for the observer who cares to pay attention to it. If the report is for a past period of time rather than a moving window of time, it won't be as valuable. A snapshot of the data stream can be attached to any periodic time report, but it won't have the same impact as the "now" reporting interfaces.

*Analytics* is the complete opposite of the sales goal. Assumptions about the topics, thresholds, conclusions, and so on are not made ahead of time; it's all exploratory. The goal of visualization for analytics is to give enough visual cues and shortcuts to allow viewers to discover interesting and useful things with some efficiency.

The result of analytics is often a more narrowly focused report. Streaming data applies well to this scenario. When the assumptions are removed, it helps to watch the data change over time to intuitively pick out trends and questions the data can answer. Analytics and the visualizations that support them are iterative; as you follow the data, each path can lead somewhere new, and the focus on that path will narrow the visibility of everything else. While analyzing data, you can move the questions you find to a report visualization and reset to start with a fresh perspective.

The analysis process doesn't end, it's a cycle of asking new questions and validating assumptions (see Figure 2-5).

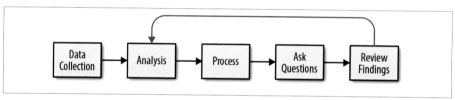

*Figure 2-5. Analysis workflow is continuous*

Figure 2-6 is an example of an interactive visualization for analysis. It doesn't give any conclusions, or answer any specific questions. It only allows exploration of the data in a way that might lead to new findings.

*Figure 2-6. An interactive visualization that does not require investigation to come to particular conclusions may lead to new questions—it's completely open-ended (source: http://bit.ly/2L3laJm)*

Understanding the intended goals and audience is critical to producing the desired result with a visualization. It wouldn't work well to show a page with moving complex data to someone passing by. It would also be ineffective to show a visualized conclusion without supporting data to an analyst who is intimately familiar with the subject matter. In both cases, you will lose your audience and the impact you hope to achieve.

A pattern I've observed over time in audiences is that something that looks too detailed will be ignored by nonspecialists, and something that looks too good will be dismissed by specialists in that data field. The assumption is that if it looks too good, it has a sales purpose, and if it looks complex, it has an analytics purpose. This doesn't need to be true—you can make an effective set of visualizations that look great, are simple enough to understand at a glance, and have the detail available for those willing to spend the extra time looking at them—but it's difficult to combat the assumptions of your audience, and it may not be worth it based on your goals. If you want to get a point across, make sure it looks great. If you want people to explore the data in detail, don't cover it up with too much presentation. Figure 2-7 is an example of a polished report dashboard. It answers specific questions with a static layout. Exploration is limited to what is intentionally presented.

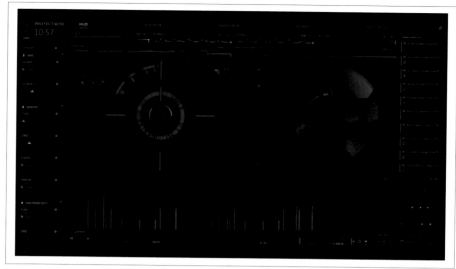

*Figure 2-7. ProtectWise (https://www.protectwise.com/) might have gone too far in building an amazing presentation—everything here has a purpose and data behind it, but it looks so good, it leaves a lot of people skeptical of its utility*

Each of the data presentation categories mentioned here can easily be further subdivided into more categories and goals. Next we will concentrate on some of the individual goals and use cases of streaming data visualizations.

# Pre-batch Analysis

Data is typically handled in large batches for efficiency and easier development. For most cases, using batches makes sense because the results would not be reviewed or acted upon any faster than the batch is processed anyway. But there are several situations where streaming data prior to or during a batch solves some problems:

- When there is critical actionable information before the next batch will run
- When a preview of the data in the next batch helps set context and verify results
- When the batch processing is complex and some problems can be observed without waiting for it to complete

The workflow in Figure 2-8 represents streaming opportunities in a batch processing system.

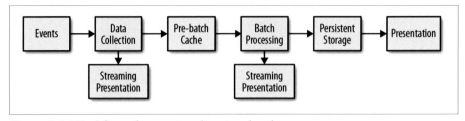

*Figure 2-8. Workflow of streaming data in a batch process*

When adding streaming data to an existing batch processing workflow, it's unnecessary to store the data again or block on anything the streaming is doing. The streaming data is intended to be fire-and-forget from the perspective of the batch processing workflow. The streaming data client will show statistics and the latest events to occur, and if it misses some, it can query them from the persistent storage or cache. There will always be more events streaming in to review.

# The Analyst Decision Queue

An *analyst queue* is a place where you present all of the information necessary to make a decision. You then treat the analyst like your most valuable data classifier. Here are a few things to consider to accomplish that:

1. Anything that can wait until later, should.

2. Automate as much as possible before presenting information to an analyst.

3. Present analysts with the decisions that are the most critical and difficult to get right with automation.

4. Attempt to correct any processing and machine learning algorithms you have based on analyst input.

5. Peer-review decisions and allow analysts to collaborate as much as possible.

Each of the steps in Figure 2-9 represents an opportunity for analyst inclusion and would benefit from their involvement.

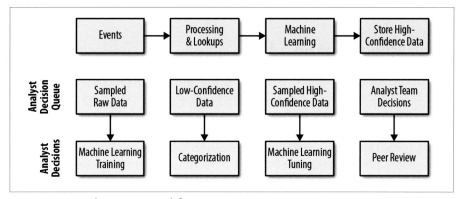

*Figure 2-9. Analyst queue workflow*

The goal is to use automation where it's best suited, and analysts where it's not. Create a process that doesn't require an army of analysts or trust the automation to do everything, but augments the analyst's role with intelligence in a complementary fashion. We will discuss this more in Chapter 9, *Streaming Analysis*.

# Data Pipeline Visualization

When you have a complex processing pipeline, it helps to know how the processes connect and how many are at each step. This can help you get a sense of where to scale bottlenecks, where items might be dropping, and what the overall health of the system is. Figure 2-10 shows a possible solution for visualizing a processing workflow as data moves across components of a system.

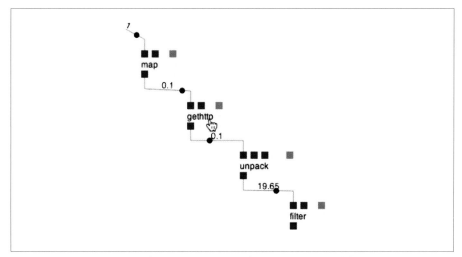

*Figure 2-10. A streaming data presentation of a processing workflow (source: http://nytlabs.com/streamtools/)*

We will discuss processing pipelines in Chapter 5.

## Show Movement on a Map

Some of the most commonly seen and most impressive streaming data visualizations are maps. Similar to seeing data move through a pipeline, seeing anything appropriate moving on a map can help viewers intuitively understand what is going on. The map can be of anything—the globe, a city, a subway, a network, or anything else that can be represented visually in this manner. If your data doesn't easily plot to physical coordinates, other types of maps may make sense. Maps of network systems are often shown in a representation of systems organized into their logical environments and routing paths. Operational intelligence can be mapped to workflows and how they relate to each other. If something moves, it can be mapped in a manner that shows where it came from and where it's going. Figure 2-11 is an interactive streaming map from Uber that uses WebGL to show streaming traffic in 3d.

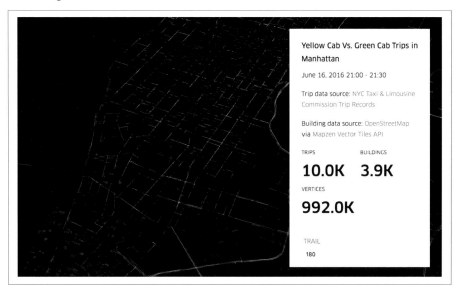

*Figure 2-11. Streaming data visualized on a map to show movement (source: http:// uber.github.io/deck.gl/#/)*

## Asking New Questions

Streaming data visualizations are best used for scenarios where you don't exactly know what questions you will ask, much less what the answers to those will be. This is when you "follow the data." This is typical in the beginning of a development process, where you have data and need to develop reporting and interfaces around it. What's unusual but useful is to continue the process of exploring the data and asking new questions. Some example questions you might ask based on streaming and visualizing the data without bias include the following:

- Where is this field expressed in my reports?
- Are we using this field as a filter?
- Is this a new trend?
- When did that value start getting used?
- Why do we have a bunch of blank values?

In answering these types of questions, you can discover problems, make more sense of your data, think of more efficient ways to process it, and more. It's really hard to predict what you can find.

> But there are also unknown unknowns—the ones we don't know we don't know.
>
> —Donald Rumsfeld

## Seeing Frequency and Order

After seeing data streaming by in any form for a while, you will get a sense of what's typical. You'll be able to notice when something is different in general, or just different for the time of day or day of week. You can get a sense of how often items will flood in as a burst instead of just seeing their running total in a batch. These are all significant things that can lead you to ask new questions and investigate. This added sense of time and frequency is one of the most significant differences in a streaming visualization. Figure 2-12 intuitively presents order and frequency of data

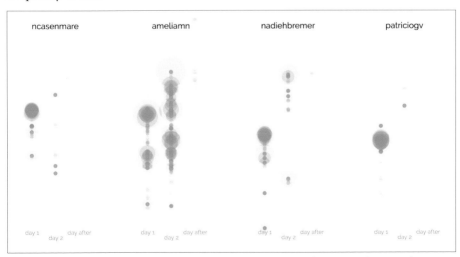

*Figure 2-12. A streaming visualization of tweets to show frequency (source: http:// vallandingham.me/openvis_tweets/)*

If multiple goals mentioned here sound like they will help you, I recommend picking one and running through everything with just that one in mind. After you are comfortable with that, you can do the same with the other goals, or you may have an idea of how to tackle several at once. Until you have the experience of trying to do some of these things, you won't have enough information to develop a solution that meets all your needs. Running through a proof of concept or three can save you a lot of frustration.

# CHAPTER 3

# Data Sources

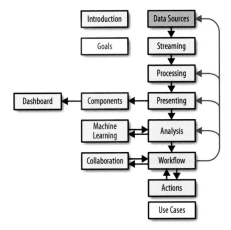

In order to visualize streaming data, you need to identify and connect to a data source. There are a few publicly available data sources that are always streaming data, such as the examples mentioned in Chapter 1, but these are unlikely to meet your goals or needs. There is a big gap between all the unexploited possibilities of streaming data and data that is actually being streamed for a purpose.

No one will know your data better than you do. This chapter will help you determine what data is worth streaming and how to access it. A lot of systems have streaming data but don't easily allow it to be used that way. After reading this chapter, you should be able to identify how you can tap into data that isn't officially streaming yet.

# Data Source Types

Any data can be streamed, but some types lend themselves better to downstream actions like visualizing than others. It's a good idea to know what you are working with prior to diving in. The easiest data to work with as a stream is atomic and structured. *Atomic* means that it has a clear beginning and end. We will refer to atomic data as "messages." *Structured* data is parsed into various fields and values with a consistent schema. A schema defines the structure for the data: what fields exist, what data they contain, and if there is any hierarchy or relationships. Structured data allows for the most mapping of visual elements to values.

The minimal structure that is applied to a message is an action. Actions or events can be categorized when nothing else is structured because the action can be appended at the time of creation based on its source. For example, the errors from a web server can be streamed as "error" actions. Even adding this minor level of structure to the data makes a big difference. Categorized actions allow a division of channels and simple statistics per action. We will define a message that has a categorized action as an "event." When most of the message is structured, we will call it a "record." Records are the ideal when processing and visualizing data. We will discuss how to get more records to work with out of messages later. Table 3-1 shows the difference between which data source types you choose to use. There is a tradeoff between volume and how machine-readable it is.

*Table 3-1. Data source comparison table*

|  | Categorized actions | Structured data |
|---|---|---|
| Message |  |  |
| Event | X |  |
| Record | X | X |

# What to Stream

Once you've identified the data you need to stream, you'll have a few options for how to stream it into the service you have chosen. Unless you already have data streaming from the source you need, you will need to build that bridge. The major areas we will consider are attaching to existing logs, event-based monitoring built into applications, and polling APIs and databases.

Each one has different challenges and advantages. In most environments, you can choose one of many locations to get to the same information. The more consistent you are in your approach to getting the data, the better it will work as an overall system. Reuse as many tools as possible, and try to pick the data collection method that is the best fit and most consistent for your solution.

Logs are the most common, but their formats will vary and they will require inline parsing. Tailing log files is the easiest way to create a new data stream to work with. Existing monitoring systems will already have a streaming data architecture that you may be able to tap into. If they have an open API, this can allow you to take advantage of already centralized, normalized, and categorized data. Similarly, if your systems already have an API for the information that you need to stream, you can poll the API for updates. This is not technically difficult if the API is able to handle the increased frequency of calls. Finally, if you have an old or simple data system that outputs only a CSV file of data, you can stream through the results after the fact. Table 3-2 compares efforts of streaming data methods

*Table 3-2. Streaming data methods*

| | Difficulty | Online | Resource intensity | Data structure |
|---|---|---|---|---|
| **Logs** | Easiest | Disconnected | | Events |
| **Monitoring** | Hardest | Connected | Lowest impact | Depends on development effort |
| **Polling** | Abstracted | | Highest impact | Structured records |
| **CSV** | Easy | Disconnected | Low impact | Flat records |

# Data Storage Considerations

The data must be stored at various stages in its life cycle. How it's stored and where has a big impact on what is possible to do with it.

Table 3-3 compares some common storage techniques. Complex environments will have several of these implemented at once. In addition to these considerations for choosing data persistence methods, you should consider what is already being used in your environment that you can leverage.

*Table 3-3. Considerations for common data persistence methods*

| Storage | Examples | Strengths | Weaknesses | Use cases |
|---|---|---|---|---|
| **Files** | Text, JSON, CSV | Portable, compressible | Not indexed for fast searching<br>Manual | Raw data<br>Data transport between systems |
| **Database** | SQL | Indexed, structured relationships<br>Fast aggregates | Extremely structured<br>Difficult to scale beyond the limitations of a single server | Relational data<br>Consistent structure |
| **Document store** | MongoDB<br>Elasticsearch<br>NoSQL | Flexible<br>Moderately scalable | Not relational<br>Slow aggregates | Inconsistent data<br>Atomic more than relational |
| **Distributed storage** | HBase<br>Cassandra | Highly scalable | Complex maintenance<br>Inefficient | Beyond the scale of other systems |

*Files* are perfect for long-term storage and moving data between systems. When a file is imported into a system, it will probably need some level of parsing and processing (see Chapter 5) in order to be used on the new system. Some systems, such as Hadoop, will allow you to keep a collection of files and work with them if they are in a certain format. It is possible to stream a file by sending a certain number of records at an interval (see "Buffering" on page 32). This can be useful when a workflow needs to occur for each record and there is an advantage to watching it occur instead of seeing the results of a large batch.

*Relational databases* are the most common method of storing data with indexes on fields that need to be referenced quickly. You can stream results out of a database using a buffer, but the most benefit can be seen from streaming the binlog of the database. The *binlog* is a record of changes, used primarily for replication. By streaming the binlog, you are able to see information as it occurs without needing to poll the database through an application or API. Streaming the binlog into a pipeline and visualizing it brings new capabilities to an established technology. You can also store results from analyst decisions back into a database.

A *document store* requires no schema to be used. A mixed set of messages with varying data and structure can be stored here. This can be a good place to cache unpredictable data before being able to process it or stream it to a client.

*Distributed storage* is an ambiguous term, but here it represents large systems built on top of something like Hadoop that are beyond the scale of most other systems. These highly redundant and scalable platforms have their own streaming technologies that they work well with, such as Kafka. The larger the scale of the streaming data, the more consideration needs to be given as to which records are most worth displaying to an analyst and when.

# Managing Multiple Sources

Your data streams and sources won't often map to your use cases. The two major considerations are the number of sources and schemas. As we saw, a schema defines the structure of the data. Applications usually require specific schemas to handle their functions and output a specific schema. When you run the same application in multiple instances, you'll have multiple sources with the same schema. When you have different applications, you'll have different schemas. This ends up being very important when processing the data. Here are scenarios to consider when you have multiple sources:

- Many to one, same schema
- Many to one, different schemas
- Many to many, different schemas

Figure 3-1 shows what the different mappings might look like for one or multiple data sources.

If you are taking advantage of streaming data in multiple applications or from different sources, you need to give some thought to how you will divide or combine the streams in such a way that they can be effectively monitored and visualized. There are a few things to consider:

Goals
> How does combining or splitting streams best suit your goals?

Schema variation
> Are the schemas the same?

Events
> Are there ways of dividing events that are more significant than by their source?

Volume
> Is the volume high enough to warrant splitting, or low enough that combining makes sense?

Examples 3-1 through 3-3 show the various methods that can be used to organize the data streams in all of the combinations shown in Figure 3-1.

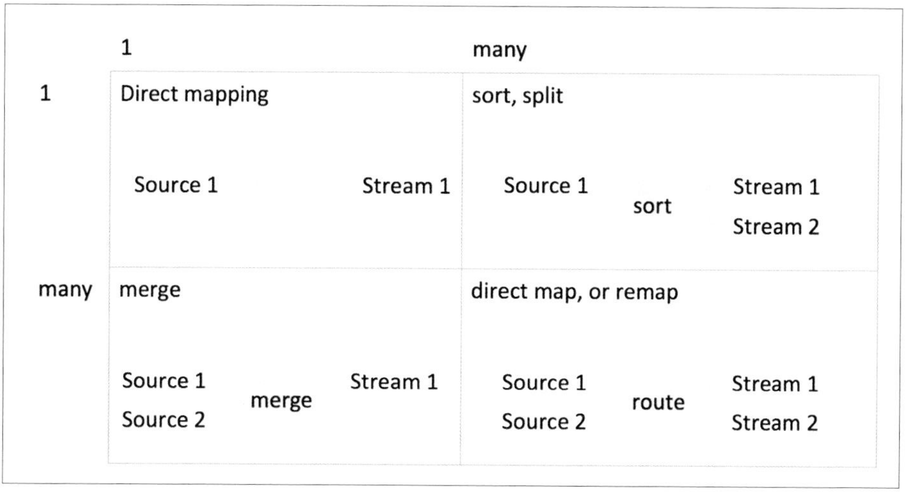

|  | 1 | many |
|---|---|---|
| 1 | Direct mapping | sort, split |
|  | Source 1 → Stream 1 | Source 1 — sort → Stream 1 / Stream 2 |
| many | merge | direct map, or remap |
|  | Source 1 / Source 2 — merge → Stream 1 | Source 1 / Source 2 — route → Stream 1 / Stream 2 |

Figure 3-1. Source-to-stream mapping

Example 3-1. Split stream, simple round-robin

```
// set stream count
var intStreams=4;
// current stream
var intCurrentStream=1;
```

```
var fnOnMessage=function(objMsg){
  // assuming this function will send to the stream specified
  fnSendMessage(intCurrentStream,objMsg);
  // update the stream pointer
  if(intCurrentStream === intStreams){
    // reset
    intCurrentStream=1;
  }else{
    //Increment
    intCurrentStream++;
  }
}
```

*Example 3-2. Stream sort/map*

```
var objMap={
  "production":1,
  "development":2,
  "staging":3,
  "certification":4
};
var fnOnMessage(objMsg){
  // assuming this function will send to the stream specified
  // map the environment data by the map
  fnSendMessage(objMap[objMsg.environment],objMsg);
}
```

*Example 3-3. Sort by schema*

```
// properties to look for in an object
var objMap={
  "ip":1,
  "url":2,
  "sha256":3,
  "regex":4
};
var arrFields=Object.keys(objMap);
var fnOnMessage(objMsg){
  var fFound=false;
  var intStream=0;
  for(var i=0;i<arrFields.length;i++){
    if(fFound===false &&
       typeof objMsg[arrFields[i]] !== 'undefined'){
       intStream=objMap[arrFields[i]];
       // stop on first one found
       fFound=true;
    }
  }
  //assuming this function will send to the stream specified
  fnSendMessage(intStream,objMsg);
}
```

Any data that is collected and useful to you can be streamed. Don't be limited by what's officially streamed. Find what you need, and then in the next chapter we'll talk about ways to attach to it.

# CHAPTER 4

# Streaming Your Data

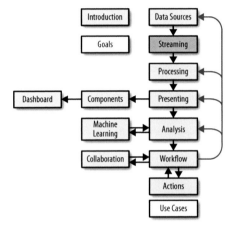

This chapter covers some specifics of how to stream data that you have identified. There are always more ways to stream data, but this covers the most common methods currently in use.

There are two important aspects to consider with any streaming data endeavor: publication and subscription. Both must be in place to effectively stream data for a visualization. Regardless of your data source, you will need to publish the data into a stream. Streams of data are often divided into channels and sometimes further divided into events. A service needs to exist to publish to, and a client needs to be connected to that service to publish events into it. This is an important detail to consider when evaluating data streaming services. First you need to get your data into the service; then you need to subscribe to a data stream. The exact method you use for this will depend on the service you choose. You will then receive the stream of data that is published, filtered by channels and events in some cases. This is the data you will be able to visualize.

Many publishers and many subscribers can be working within the same data stream. This is one of the advantages of streaming data: it lends itself well to a distributed architecture. You could have a large collection of servers publish their errors into a data stream and have multiple subscribers to that data stream for different purposes. Subscribers could include an operations dashboard, event-based fixit scripts, alert generators, and interactive analysis tools. It is also possible to have the service and publishing components combined. This can be easy to deploy but limits options on combining information from multiple sources. web socketd is a good example of a service combined with a publisher that is easy to set up and creates a single publisher to a data stream.

Key things to consider in choosing a service for streaming data are cost, scalability, maintenance, security, and any special requirements you have, like programming language support. Table 4-1 lists some popular examples.

*Table 4-1. Example services*

| Service | Licensing | Notes |
| --- | --- | --- |
| Socket.IO | Open source | A popular and easy standard for building your own streaming. |
| SocketCluster | Open source | A distributed version of Socket.IO for scalability. |
| websocketd | Open source | Utility to stream anything from a console. |
| WebSockets | Standard | A standard supported by most browsers. The current baseline for all streaming services. |
| Pusher | Commercial | A complete streaming server solution. Paid service. |
| PubNub | Commercial | A complete streaming server solution. Paid service. |

# How to Stream Data

A few scenarios can cover most needs in streaming data. We'll look at each of these in turn:

- Using a publish/subscriber channel or message queue
- Streaming file contents
- Emitting messages from something that is already streaming
- Streaming from the console
- Polling a service or API

A publish/subscriber channel is a mechanism for publishing events into a channel to be consumed by all those who subscribe to it. This is a pattern intended for streaming data and is also known as *pub/sub*. Pub/sub libraries will handle all of the connections for you, but you may need to buffer the data yourself.

Streaming file contents may sound odd because they're static and can be run through a program to analyze at will or in a batch. But you may still want to do this if your file is the beginning of a workflow of multiple components that you want to monitor as it occurs. For example, if you have a long list of URLs in a file to run against several APIs and services, it may take a while to get the results back. When you do, it would be a shame to find out that an error had occurred or you'd gathered the wrong information, or they'd all ended up redirecting to the same spot. These are things that would stand out if you were streaming the lines of the file to a service and seeing the results as they returned.

To stream the contents of a file, you can either have a service hold the file open and stream the contents at an interval per record or dump the contents of the file into a service and allow it to keep it in memory while it emits the records at an interval. If the file is below a record count that can comfortably fit into memory —maybe less than 1 GB of records—then the second method is preferred. If the file is much larger than you want to store in memory, keep it open and stream at the interval you need. If you are able to work with the file in memory, you have the added advantage of being able to do some sorts on the data before sending. Papa Parse (*http://papaparse.com/*) is an easy-to-implement library that you can use to stream your files. It allows you to attach each line to an event so that you can stream it:

```
Papa.parse(bigFile, {
  worker: true,
  step: function(results) {
      YourStreamingEventFunction();
  }
});
```

Many applications stream data between components. Many of them have a convenient spot to tap into and emit events as they occur. For example, you can stream a MySQL binlog that's used for replication by using an app that watches the binlog as if it were a replication server and emits the information as JSON. One such library for MySQL and Node.js is ZongJi (*http://bit.ly/2xrzuJV*):

```
var zongji = new ZongJi({ /* ... MySQL Connection Settings ... */ });

// Each change to the replication log results in an event
zongji.on('binlog', function(objMsg) {
  fnOnMessage(objMsg);
})
```

Similar libraries can be found for other data storage technologies and anything that has multiple components.

Streaming from a console gets back to the original streaming data example of watching tailed logs scroll by. By turning a scrolling console into a streaming data source, you can add a lot of processing and interaction to the data instead of just watching it fly by. websocketd (*http://websocketd.com/*) is a convenient little open source application that will allow you to turn anything emitted in a console into a WebSocket with the lines sent to the console as messages. These will need to be parsed into some sort of structure to be useful. You can create multiple instances that run in the background or as services. This can be very effective to get a good idea of what's going on and what's useful, but may not be a long-term solution.

To start `websocketd` and create a stream, use a shell command like the following:

```
websocketd --port=8080 ./script-with-output.sh
```

Then connect to the `websocketd` stream in JavaScript:

```
// setup WebSocket with callbacks
var ws = new WebSocket('ws://localhost:8080/');
ws.onmessage = function(objMsg) {
  fnOnMessage(objMsg);
};
```

Finally, polling an API is an attractive option because APIs are everywhere. They are the most prolific method of data exchange between systems. There are several types of APIs, but most of them will return either a list of results or details on a record returned in a previous response. Both of these work well in an interactive streaming data visualization client. The API polling workflow is as follows:

1. Call the API for a list.
2. Stream the list to the client at a reasonable interval.
3. Run any processing and filters that fit your goals.
4. For any records that pass the conditions to get details, make the details API call.
5. Show the results of the details API call as they return.
6. When you reach the end of the list, make another API call for the list.
7. Stream only the new items from the API call.
8. Repeat.

Using one of the options described here, you can stream just about anything you would like to and get a live view of what is transpiring.

# Buffering

If we suppose that an analyst can understand up to 20 records per second while intently watching the screen, it may not make sense to fly past that limit when data is coming in faster than that. *Buffering* allows data to be cached before going to the next step; it means you can intelligently stream records to a downstream process instead of being at the mercy of the speed of the incoming data. This makes a big difference in the following instances:

---

- When the data is streaming in much faster than it can be consumed
- When the data source is unpredictable, and the data can come in large bursts
- When the data comes in all at once but needs to be streamed out

Cross these scenarios with the likely data needs of an analyst, and you start to have some logic that maintains the position of the analyst's view within the buffer as well as the buffer itself. The analyst's views in the buffer are

- Newest data (data as it arrives)
- Oldest data (data about to leave the buffer)
- Samples of data (random selections from the buffer)

Any of these buffer views can be mixed with conditions on what records are worth viewing to filter out anything unneeded for the current task. To meet all of these conditions, the following rules can be applied in your buffering logic:

- Put all incoming data into a large cache.
- If the data is larger than the cache, decide what to do with it. You can

  1. Replace the entire contents of the cache with the new data.
  2. Accept a portion of the new data if you have not seen enough of the previous data.
  3. Grow the cache.

- Set the viewable items within the cache to correspond to the buffer view required by the analyst.
- When new data is added at a rate that can be easily consumed, move it into the cache and the views where appropriate.
- When data is added too quickly to be consumed intelligently, trickle it in at a pace that is suitable.
- When data is not arriving at all, start streaming records that haven't been seen yet.

Figure 4-1 shows the relationship between a changing cache and moving views within it.

*Figure 4-1. Buffer views and movement in relation to a cache for streaming data*

# Streaming Best Practices

These are guidelines to consider implementing in your data streaming strategy:

- Stream data as something that is fire-and-forget, not as blocking for any process or as a reliable record.

- Use a protocol that encrypts the data in transport for anything sensitive. Without an encrypted transport such as WSS, a simple packet sniffer can see the data in plain text passively.

- Create multiple channels or queues to organize streams of data. Each channel can be assigned a different purpose and set of processes.

- Don't mix data schemas in the same channel. This makes it much easier to process anything within that channel.

- Separate analyst feedback events into a separate channel. This helps with the processes of team collaboration and peer review, and can also help prevent feedback loops.

- Consider a distributed and coordinated service if your scale goes beyond what a single server can handle. In some instances, having multiple clients connected and getting different results at different times causes confusion (and worse).

- Use technologies that abstract the specific streaming protocol and allow multiple protocols to be used easily and interchangeably.

Going from not streaming data to streaming data might be the largest obstacle in producing a working solution that you can show to others to get feedback. It will require some access to data or systems that are not typical. If you can get a plug-in or official feature to stream what you need, that's always your best bet. If not, you can still connect at the points mentioned here.

# CHAPTER 5

# Processing Streaming Data for Visualization

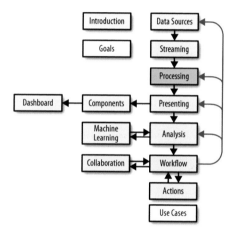

Processing data is the most common operation mentioned in this book. There are specific considerations to bear in mind when processing streaming data to be visualized.

## Batch Processing

*Batch processing* is the most common approach for handling high volumes of data. The process of batching means that data will be cached somewhere to be processed at intervals. The processing interval is chosen according to the data's significance and the ability to take actions on it. Processing daily batches overnight is by far the most common approach, but daily batch processing falls short when there are significant events that may have occurred almost 24 hours earlier by the time the report is reviewed by a person. An indicator that your brand has been mimicked publicly for malicious purposes would be an instance where every minute counts. In order to deal with this, hourly batch processing is often used. Most applications will not process batches more often than hourly because of perceived limitations in being able to act on the data any faster. Another reason for not processing batches too often is that it's a complex process and has the potential to not finish before processing of the next batch begins, causing a backlog.

The process that runs at the chosen interval will query the data from where it's stored in order to create the aggregate statistics predetermined to be significant. These statistics will be saved for later visualization in an application. The application that shows the aggregate data in a dashboard is usually the first view someone has of the data. The high-level view is used to determine what is worth drilling down into and seeing in more detail. When record details are requested, they are retrieved to be shown in addition to the original information.

# Inline Processing

*Inline processing* is less common than batch processing because its immediate event-based approach is more complex and it's susceptible to issues during spikes of activity that are beyond its capability to keep up with. With this method, each event will kick off a chain of decisions and processing before storing a result or displaying it to a person. This approach lends itself well to visualizing streaming data because it shows the required information rapidly and can at least show the amount of data at a frequency that a person can understand.

Any process that is complex or mature enough will require both inline and batch processing models. Visualizing streaming data effectively requires both approaches to complement each other. Microbatches are required to keep up with the data volume, while inline processing will get secondary information on a selective set of filtered, throttled, and vetted results of the microbatches.

# Processing Patterns

Many of the frameworks for streaming data mentioned in this book offer an easy way to process the data inline. You may need to do something more custom to achieve what you are after, though. If you are streaming data for the purpose of analytics, the more you can process inline and show to the analyst to help them understand a pattern or make a decision, the more effective their analysis will be. There are a few principles and patterns to keep in mind when programming for streaming data:

- Use microservices for calling information inline.

- Assume information returned will be asynchronous and nonblocking.
- Assume everything is a batch of data, with batch sizes of whatever occurs in ~1–60 seconds.
- Not all processes need to occur for all events.
- Stream-processing ecosystems can be heterogeneous.
- Separate data dispatch from data processing for scalability.
- Caching can help reduce redundant processing.
- Store the original event before inline processing for visualization.
- Route events to their respective processing pipelines as early as possible.
- Processing flows can be cyclical.
- Each step and component can be displayed if needed.
- Consider using the pub/sub pattern.

In a microservices architecture, functions are broken into small atomic components that can be called separately. Each one is ignorant of the larger environment and can run independently. This approach is a foundation component for a complex, flexible ecosystem that is highly redundant and scalable without being difficult to monitor and maintain.

For example, if you have a stream of URLs that you need to process, you may need to do some processing, parsing, and gathering of statistics. All of this can be done in separate components. You may also need to crawl each URL, grab some screenshots, and look up some third-party information about the history, reputation, and risk of visiting the site. After gathering all this information, you might want to visualize it quickly in order to make a decision about each URL. If you were to perform all of these tasks inline, you would have a process that takes the maximum amount of time because nothing would be done in parallel. If something failed, everything that had successfully completed would be lost (unless cached). In a single all-encompassing process, you also have a mix of resource requirements and have difficulty knowing if any components are down until they fail.

The microservices architecture is commonly used to avoid these issues, and is used today in many processes that don't involve streaming data as well. Breaking out each component into something that can be called independently makes it easier to constantly monitor each of them. You can also call them from multiple events or several times in the same event without needing to repeat the code. You can scale the components separately and with different resources. In our example, the screenshots and crawling may take a while to return, while the other components could return very quickly. With the microservices architecture, you can have several screenshot and crawl components in a pool ready to be called, but only enough of the other components to be redundant. You can call all of these components at the same time and wait for all of them to return to be displayed, or show information as it's available. Whether you wait to display everything at once or show results as they're completed should depend on how much is required by an interactive analyst to make a decision.

Figure 5-1 illustrates an example microservices architecture, showing independent scaling of services, monitoring, and streaming through modularity and distribution.

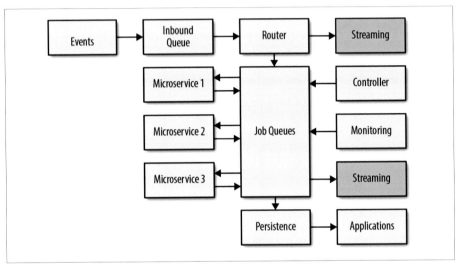

*Figure 5-1. Example microservices architecture*

Streaming data is often assumed to be completely event-based. This is true up to a certain volume and scale, but once the number of events to be processed reaches a certain level, or if a significant overhead can be saved by processing multiple events at once, there is a need to create small batches defined by practical limits. Example 5-1 shows how this can be done.

*Example 5-1. Processing in batches of one second*

```
var arrBatch=[];
var intTimeStart=Date.now();
var intLimit=1000;
var fnOnMessage=function(objMsg){
  var intNow=Date.now();
  arrBatch.unshift(objMsg);
  if(intNow>intTimeStart+intLimit){
    intTimeStart=intNow;
    fnProcessBatch();
  }
}
```

```
var fnProcessBatch=function(){
  for(var i=0;i<arrBatch.length;i++){
    // process each record
  }
}
```

For visualizing streaming data, the practical limits are somewhere between one second and one minute per batch—this is the approximate amount of time that someone watching the information needs to understand and get any intuitive insight from it. People can definitely make subsecond decisions, but when there are dozens of records per second or more, it's a pretty safe assumption that this is beyond the upper limit of human speed. Find a batch size/time that works best for your goals.

Even with a nice scalable microservices architecture, it's easy to have more events than you can or need to process occurring across all of your components. In our URLs example, if you do the fast lookup for history and other third-party data, you may be able to make a determination without a screenshot or crawling. And you may be able to bypass a decision altogether based on some data or the time elapsed since a previous related decision. Anything you can do to quickly account for events and then filter them out will gain efficiency in both processing and analyst time.

When you are gathering your components to be used in stream processing, they need to be compatible only to the point that their inputs and outputs can be easily normalized to work with each other. The language they are written in, the data store behind them, licensing, and many of the other obstacles in software development can be avoided by using the components as modules.

In order to coordinate all of the processing that needs to occur for all of the events and what to do when they return, you'll need a controller of some sort. It may be necessary to create a separate service for dispatching. The dispatcher will see all events and act as a load balancer between controllers. A lot of common libraries can handle this capability at scale, including message queue systems, like RabbitMQ and ZeroMQ.

In most data processes, there is a lot of redundancy. In the URL example, you may get a lot of the same domains with some slight URL variations, if you aren't seeing complete duplicates. If each of the components is able to keep some cache of its responses, they can return results quickly and move on to the next thing that needs to be processed. If you chart the unique versus duplicate requests to each component over a month, you will see a clear point of diminishing returns in terms of caching. This exercise is recommended for the most commonly called components of the highest resource intensity. Common caching options include a fast database or an in-memory key/value store like Memcached. Checking the cache will add some overhead to your components' processing time, and for this reason it's recommended to not have a larger cache than can be quickly searched in memory or at memory speeds. It's essential to ensure that all cache mechanisms have an intentional method to prevent them from expanding beyond their useful size and lifetime.

There is most likely some redundancy between the streaming data processing you need to do and the normal batch processing that you'd need to do for any longer-term reporting. This can create the temptation to wait until all the information is gathered and store it later. The events may not reoccur, though, so it's important to record them however you need to first—even if it just means accounting for some benign and common event before throwing it out. Any of the inline processing components that are called can add data to later be referenced by any longer-term process that occurs.

If you have multiple processing flows (a set of components to be used in a specific sequence), the most efficient thing to do is to separate them as soon as possible. If possible, separate them at an architecture level: have different events point to different dispatching queues. If a single data source creates multiple types of events that require processing, you will need to include that logic after they are all in the queue.

Some components or processes can also be event sources. In the URLs example, after crawling and discovering referenced or related URLs, those may also be submitted into the queue to be processed. This is another time that a cache is important. If the crawler keeps some basic data on what it has processed recently, it can prevent an infinite loop.

Even if a number of processes are required before an analyst can make a decision, there are a few reasons you may want to present information in the middle of the processing flow. It can offer insight into what's being done with the data, and it can let you see gaps or errors in the processing logic. It can also be significant for knowing when components need to scale or be tuned based on their frequency of use and time to return results.

# Lookups

Streaming data shouldn't exist in isolation. Certain events will justify a data lookup from another source, and sometimes it's even worth creating your own lookup source, such as a screenshot of a website. Once you have processed, categorized, and prioritized the data, you should be able to use those results to determine what to investigate next. Any time you require more information to make a timely decision, making a secondary lookup for that information may be worthwhile.

This is especially useful when you need to display something to an analyst to enable them to make an intuitive call. A good example of this is phishing scams.

*Phishing* is a term used for a type of attack where someone does whatever they can to convince you to click a malicious link. The attacker will typically impersonate a legitimate service such as a bank or online service and give you a compelling reason to pay attention. Many characteristics of phishing can be automatically determined, such as use of a domain name that is visually similar to but not exactly the same as that of a popular service. For example, *Bank0fAmerica.com* looks close enough to *BankOfAmerica.com* to not stand out at first glance (the O is replaced with a zero); if there is a domain like this available, an attacker can register it to deceive people. If you were streaming data for the purpose of sifting through potentially malicious links, something like this should get a very high priority.

It can be hard to make a decision by looking at the link alone, though. The next step would be to go to the domain to take a look, but this is not always possible or advisable when looking at potentially malicious domains, and it can take a lot of accumulated time and effort when you're looking at hundreds per day. This is where a data lookup comes in handy. You can set up a safe system to get a screenshot automatically when the automatically collected data justifies it, and display it to an analyst for the intuitive call. Whatever decision the analyst comes to can be saved with the data and used in further processing or training of supervised machine learning models. This workflow of processing and doing lookups may go through several iterations before anything is displayed to an analyst, but the concept remains the same.

## Lookup Types

There are three types of lookups: API, database, and application.

*API lookups* are the most frequently implemented. APIs are the most common interface for data exchange, whether internal or external to the organization. Once you know what you are looking to get more information on, you send it to the appropriate API and handle the response. API calls take a while. They likely won't be able to keep up with the streaming data if used too frequently. This is why it makes sense to filter and a process a stream before making an API call, so that it can be narrowed down to whatever justifies it. For example, if looking at Wikimedia edits, you may be interested in looking up only more information about any edits that were blocked and why.

The following example shows how to do an API lookup for IP data related to the IP address we get in a record. ThreatCrowd is a popular place to look up IP data for free and has an easy-to-use API. Gathering this type of information before a person or system needs to look at it helps a lot—it saves them time looking it up and immediately gives them some context to go with it. The code in Example 5-2 is specific to AngularJS.

*Example 5-2. Sample API lookup*

```
var strIp = objMsg.ip;
var objConfig={
  'url':
  "https://www.threatcrowd.org/searchApi/v2/ip/report/?ip="+strIp
};
if(strIp!=='127.0.0.1'){
  $http(objConfig).then(
    function fnSuccess(objResponse){
    // add the API response to the data
    objMsg.api={objResponse};
  },
    function fnError(objResponse){}
  );
}
```

*Database lookups* are required when you have previously stored information that is relevant to a current decision. This is usually related to history. If you need to decide whether something is typical, you need to keep history and compare to it. You can connect your app directly to a database or put a small API in front of it and do something similar to the previous example.

*Application lookups* are quite varied, depending on the purpose and capability of the application. The difference between an application and an API lookup is that the application will not return an immediate result. This means that it either needs to be polled for information or needs to create its own data stream for the results.

# Normalizing Events

When data is being analyzed for outliers, it helps to have it be as consistent as possible during normal operation. It might be normal not to get a field when it's blank. Instead of not showing that field at all, assigning a default value can make things align better downstream. Example 5-3 shows one approach for this.

*Example 5-3. Normalize the data structure, add defaults when missing*

```
var objTemplate={ip:'127.0.0.7',system:'unknown'};
var arrTemplateKeys=Object.keys(objTemplate);
var fnOnMessage=function(objMsg){
  for(var i=0;i<arrTemplateKeys.length;i++){
    if(typeof objMsg[arrTemplateKeys[i]] === 'undefined'){
      // this expected field doesn't exist, add it with default val
      objMsg[arrTemplateKeys[i]]=objTemplate[arrTemplateKeys[i]];
    }
  }
}
```

Another type of normalization could be in the values that need to be compared. The most common example is time. It's a common practice to store and transmit all data with timestamps in UTC. If this isn't done for some reason, it's a good idea to translate the timestamps before the data is used for statistics and visualizations.

# Extracting Value

You can have data streaming and being visualized and still not make very good use of it. It can be an overwhelming blast of incoherent information that makes you question the wisdom of streaming data to look at. This is a hurdle that often discourages people. Although visualization of streaming data has been avoided for so long, you can gain a lot of insight by performing some simple exercises. Within a few steps, you can make the data easier to digest and have a better understanding of its possibilities. These can be considered ingredients to be used in the processing components discussed in the preceding chapter. A lot of libraries do this type of thing. In the next section, we will use an open source one that will be easy to show examples from that can be found online. its purpose is to define these simple transformations in a set of easily interpreted JSON definitions. You can pass batches of records in as an array of JSON records along with a small config, and it will return the modified collection of records. One advantage of using a library like this is you can embed it into your applications and exchange portable configurations.

The processing examples shown next are logically straightforward. They allow data to be added, removed, or transformed based on easily defined conditions. This library (and easily defined logic for processing JSON data) can be used to accomplish a lot, but you may want to add other things to your processing that are more complex. You can use machine learning–trained classifiers or even developed algorithms to score and classify the data before showing it to an analyst. If these are things you would do anyway, it helps to show the results of the automated decisions along with the other data to the analyst to make decisions and find issues with the classification and scores. These new values can also be used with the processing rules mentioned. For example, you may have a classifier look at a URL string and make a decision about how suspicious it looks based on its various characteristics, and a guess as to what type of content will be behind it. We will talk about machine learning more in Chapter 12.

Besides just updating the data, a separate score that is unique to presenting the data can be added. This score might indicate how interesting the data is for an analyst to look at. This will allow you to do some client-side sorting by interest score and keep records in a queue for an analyst to address.

# The JSON Collection Decorator

The JSON Collection Decorator (*http://bit.ly/2Ji46SE*) is a free open source library with a particularly utilitarian name:

- *JSON* is a common data format. It's lightweight, allows hierarchy, and works well with JavaScript.
- A *collection* is a group of objects, like a batch of records.
- *Decoration* is a term used for taking an object such as a record and passing it through some functions to add, remove, or modify its properties.

A lot of similar libraries are available on Git, but this one can serve as a working example of how you can process small batches of streaming data inline. If you choose another library for this function, look for the following qualities:

- Able to take a batch of records at once.
- Records need to be looped through only once, even if there are multiple conditions and actions.
- Filtered records are removed before the rest of the processing, so they aren't decorated unnecessarily.
- Able to match multiple conditions before performing an action.
- Actions can be performed on different properties than the conditions.
- Multiple actions can be performed per condition.

The difficult balance to find with this set of functions is between performance, capability, and flexibility.

Example 5-4 illustrates how you can use the JSON Collection Decorator to process a batch of records.

*Example 5-4. Use of JSON Collection Decorator*

```
var objConfig={
   filters:[
     { path:"path.to.key",op:"eq",val:"value to match" }
   ]
,decorate:[
    {
      find:[{ path:"path.to.key",op:"eq",val:"value to match" }]
      ,do:[{ path:"path.to.key",act:"set",val:"value to set" }]
    },{
      ,find:{ path:"path.to.key",op:"eq",val:"value to match" }
      ,do:{path:"path.to.key",act:"stack"
        ,val:"value to add to array" }
    }
```

```
]
}

arrResults = decorate(objConfig,arrCollection);
```

# Processing Checklist

Here are some common tasks in the processing of a data stream:

1. Count anything that you want to account for later before filtering.
2. Filter out uninteresting records.
3. Filter out unimportant or consistent fields.
4. Parse the data types found.
5. Extract data.
6. Categorize based on content.

Let's go through these step by step.

Getting counts for things sounds like a no-brainer—it's the simplest possible statistic. However, it's often forgotten prior to filtering or throttling. It's important to know what your totals are so that you can reference them when you have more granular counts of things later that you kept.

Next, filter out records that don't offer you any insights:

```
{filters:[
  { path:"path.to.key",op:"eq",val:"value to filter by" }
]}
```

Now that you have counts of these records, it makes sense to display the counts instead of the records. All you need to do is assign them a label that accurately describes what the counts will represent.

Now, filter fields that have no variance or value:

```
{decorate:[{
 find:[{ path:"path.to.key",op:"eq",val:"value to match" }]
,do:[{ path:"path.to.key",act:"remove" }]
}]}
```

Records often contain so much information that it can be difficult to even see one record on a screen at a time. This is when filtering fields makes a big difference. After you filter out the fields you don't need at the moment, you can digest the rest of the record more easily. When filtering fields, be careful not to filter out anomalies. If a field is unused but always listed, it's safe to filter, but if it just commonly has the same value, make the filter conditional on it being that value so you can still see when it's different.

Next, parse data types that can benefit from it. A lot of data has subcomponents that can be valuable as statistics if separated. For example, several components of a URL can be significant separately. A URL contains a protocol, domain or host, path, and query string, which itself has key/value pairs. Some URLs will also contain authentication credentials. You can parse URLs with the JSON Collection Decorator as follows:

```
{decorate:[{
 find:[{ path:"path.to.key",op:"eq",val:"value to match" }]
 ,do:[{ path:"path.to.key",act:"parseUrl" }]
}]}
```

Anything that can quickly be parsed for valuable subcomponents is worthy of the effort for later use.

Then extract data from any files that are referenced. The metadata record you get for a file is rarely a complete set of all the valuable data available. There is a lot of information within files that should be contained within a record if useful, and if it isn't, you'll need to extract it. For example, images often have geographic coordinates embedded in them. You'll want to know what kind of file the operating system sees the file as, and if there are any certificates or origin information. If the file is a package, you'll need to extract it and create records for the files it contains. If you are looking at files for security purposes, you'll need to get hashes for the files.

Finally, content categorization is useful for knowing what processing workflows to apply to your data. There are a lot of methods for content categorization, from regular expressions (regexes) to machine learning. The more unstructured data there is, the more sophisticated the process will be to categorize it. Content categories can be things like "support, bug, question, complaint, comment" or "simple, complex, ludicrous." It all depends on the context of the data and what useful categorizations you can derive from it. Here's an example:

```
{decorate:[{
 find:[
   { path:"path.to.key",op:"eq",val:"value to match" }
   ,{ path:"path.to.key",op:"eq",val:"value to match" }
 ]
 ,do:[{ path:"status",act:"set",val:"ludicrous" }]
}]}
```

# Streaming Statistics

An important and distinct consideration when keeping statistics for streaming data is to try to keep the statistics in a cumulative fashion as much as possible. If every time you add an item to an array you need to evaluate the whole array to recalculate the statistics you need, as in Example 5-5, you will hit scalability limits much faster than if you keep the information as you go.

*Example 5-5. Typical stats processing in JavaScript*

```javascript
// define what's being pushed into the array
var intData=42;
// add an element to the array
arrData.push(intData);
// then use a function to get the stats you need; this uses loDash
intMax = _.max(arrData);
intMin = _.min(arrData);
intSum = _.sum(arrData);
intMean = _.mean(arrData);
```

When you are visualizing streaming data, you often need to show the current values as well as how those values relate to a larger context. This means you need to keep basic statistics up-to-date for presentation. If you use the typical process just shown for each record added, you will be looping through your entire array of items for every record, times the number of stats you are getting. That's a lot of processing for a simple task. If it needs to be done hundreds or thousands of times per second, the system processing the data might not be able to keep up. Consider the approach shown in Example 5-6 as an alternative.

*Example 5-6. Cumulative stats in JavaScript*

```javascript
// define what's being pushed into the array
var intData=42;
// update the stats
intCount++;
intSum=intSum+intData;
if(intData > intMax){ intMax=intData; }
if(intData < intMin){ intMin=intData; }
intMean = intSum/intCount;
```

This will produce the same statistics but not require any looping through the array in order to accomplish it. These types of small savings add up rapidly when processing needs to be done per record and the arrays of information stored are large. This approach also allows you to keep stats that outlive your array in case you need to keep that at a fixed size or within limits. If you have a lot of these processes running in parallel, you can have them occasionally reconcile with each other and decide who has the max, the min, etc., all without the costly processing of looping through all of the data.

# Types of Statistics

These are some basic statistics to consider keeping track of as data streams rather than calculating them on demand:

- Basic statistics (min, max, average, quartiles)
- Comparison of values
- Frequency of values
- Cardinality of values
- Co-occurrence of values
- Statistics within time windows

*Basic statistics* are fast and easy to get. They are useful for so many unexpected things that it's a good idea to keep track of them whenever possible. They are also nice to display on their own. When you see individual values, it helps a lot to know how those compare to the rest.

*Comparing values* within a record is a good way to quickly get some insights. With the Wikimedia data, it's pretty significant if an edit of a page is larger than the original page. This means that the edit represents a large overhaul or infusion of content. This deserves some recognition over other edits that might affect a fraction of a percent of the content.

*Frequency of values* can quickly tell you how common a given value is. A more complex iteration on frequency would be some time pattern analysis. This could help you understand that while a value is common overall, it is not for the time period seen.

*Cardinality of values* helps you to understand how varied the data is. It makes a big difference in deciding how to present data. If you have 3 to 12 unique values, it might be a good idea to compare them in a bar chart; if you have thousands, a bar chart will not work very well.

*Co-occurrence of values* is a useful and simple statistic to show the intersection of values. If you are getting source and destination information in your records, simply listing the top sources and the top destinations is OK, but listing the top source-to-destination combinations is much more valuable and can give a very different result.

*Statistics in time windows* will help with time pattern analysis. Streaming data is about what's happening now. Statistically, what represents "now" is a matter of scope. The current year is "now," but that's probably too large of a scope to be relevant. A useful time window for streaming data is usually less than one day, maybe hourly. Time windows can also be event-based such as the beginning and end of a show. Statistics within these time windows can be used for a historical comparison of the current window to previous ones.

# Record Context Checklist

Some broad things to consider in providing context for your record data are as follows:

- Status
- Priority
- Comparison of values to statistics

Determining a status for the record is useful for a complex workflow. This especially applies when the status is not something that can always be determined from the data originally provided but is derived from data that's added and interpreted. The status can determine where a record goes next in a workflow.

Priority can be based on a number of things, such as severity, confidence, and status. It is usually used for ordering in a queue, whether automated or interactive. Priority can be used to make sure the most important items are processed before any that can wait. This is the primary method to override a purely time-based first come, first served ordering of processing.

Comparing values to statistics will give you additional information as to where a record fits within a larger context. It can be good to know how close a value is to a minimum, maximum, or average for the existing time frame.

# Scaling Data Streams

After you have applied the necessary data manipulations, you'll have reduced the data down to what is worth displaying; you have a priority to order it in, and enough information to give fast visual cues to quickly digest. These are the things that start to make the streaming data consumable and useful by someone monitoring it. If after all of this you still have too much data, however, you may need to apply extra methods to scale it to something manageable.

Scaling the data should be looked at only after all intelligent options have been exhausted. It's always better to intelligently decide which records you view and where they are in the larger context. If the scale of the data makes that too impractical, consider the following comparison of methods to keep up with processing large volumes of data as they are generated (Table 5-1).

*Sampling* is the process of randomly grabbing every *n*th record (see Example 5-7). This can allow you to work with a more manageable scale and know what that scale is. The more records you skip in sampling, the less relevant the retained data is.

*Table 5-1. Comparison table of methods to process subsets of data*

| | Known scale | Relevance |
|---|---|---|
| **Sampling** | X | Depends on sample rate |
| **Throttling** | | Depends on whether caps are reached |
| **Hardware-bound** | | Depends on whether caps are reached |
| **Dynamic** | X | Best possible |

*Example 5-7. Sampling logic*

```
var intSample=10;
var intCount=0;
// call the sampling function every time
var fnSample=function(objMsg){
  intCount++;
  if( intCount%intSample===0){
    // the nth count, fire the function to process
    fnOnMessage(objMsg);
  }
};
```

*Throttling* (Example 5-8) puts a cap on the amount of data that is digested in a given time frame—it might be something like 1,000 records per second. This is less preferred than sampling because you don't know how many records there are in total. You cannot multiply the number of records kept to get an estimate of the total. You may be able to be more selective about what you keep and what you don't, though; you can keep a certain number of each type of record, or be selective about what records you keep after the cap is reached.

*Example 5-8. Throttle logic*

```
var intCap=1000;
var intCount=0;
var intStart=Date.now();
// call the throttling function every time
var fnThrottle=function(objMsg){
  var intNow=Date.now();
  // see if it's in a new time increment
  if(intNow>intStart+1000){ intStart=intNow; intCount=0; }
  else{ intCount++; }
  if( intCount < intCap){
    // only run if under the cap per time period
    fnOnMessage(objMsg);
  }
};
```

*Hardware-bound* scaling means that the limits depend on how much the hardware you are running on can handle. Without any other limits set, this is how processes run. If the applications and hardware are able to process all the data, you get everything. If the hardware cannot keep up with the data volume, you get an unpredictable percentage of the total data. The worst part about this is not knowing when the complete data was received and, when you get only a portion, how much of the total that portion represents.

Finally, *dynamic scaling* can be used to get the most data at the most predictable scale. This approach adjusts the throttling or sampling rate based on variables such as how many records are waiting to be processed in a queue. The key thing is to know what method is being used when, in order to make predictions and appropriate comparisons where possible. It's difficult to compare data from a throttled data source where caps are reached to a complete source. A lot of assumptions need to be made that are more appropriately explored in a deeper study of statistics.

Here are a few guidelines to keep in mind if you need to scale your data:

- First, you need to know the limits of your hardware for processing the records.
- Set the throttled amount to a comfortable value under that limit.
- When that limit is reached, switch to sampling. Sample at the lowest rate possible, keeping more records than you toss, and adjust as required, always keeping track of the sample rate.
- Set a throttle cap only as a safety stop to prevent the system from becoming unresponsive. Hopefully, this cap will never be reached, or reached only while the dynamic sampling rate is being adjusted.
- Allow the sampling rate to be reduced as well.
- Keep track of the sampling rates and of whether caps were ever reached (and when).

# Presenting Processing

The preparation of data for use in downstream systems and for presentation is a significant part of business. So far, we have talked about the processing required in order to present data to an analyst with as much information as possible to enable them to quickly make a decision. A few things specific to processing deserve consideration as well:

- Presenting where data being shown is situated within the larger processing pipeline
- Presenting any significant routes taken due to processing decisions

- Having a streaming data visualization for a complex processing ecosystem

The moment at which you see a record may not be the end of its trip through a processing pipeline. It can be useful to stream data to a client from multiple points within a larger ecosystem. When doing so, it's good to know where that data is within that context. You can either display the relevant information with the data, or associate it by its position within a layout (see Figure 5-2; layouts are discussed later in the book). Both may be required when there is a very complex pipeline. The layout will be a linear association, and any more detailed context would need to be in the data itself.

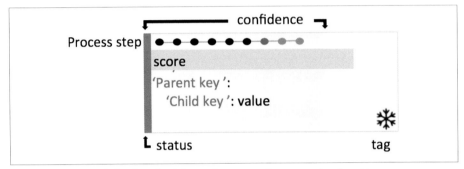

*Figure 5-2. Record displayed with a reference to its processing location*

A lot of decisions are made within a processing pipeline. Values, history, and other factors can influence what needs to be done with the data. When these decisions are made, it's good to present these decision forks to the analyst. The person looking at the data might not immediately know that certain records are processed by a different set of rules when they have values that meet certain criteria. Adding this information can help a lot in a critical situation. The indicator can be simple, such as "Bypassed for download, in cache," or even shorter than that as long as the analyst has something to quickly reference that reveals more detail. Providing this information could allow an analyst to quickly resubmit something to go down a different processing path, or prompt them to adjust future processing rules to have a new route on a new condition. Without having that context displayed, they wouldn't have the opportunity.

The processing pipeline is essential to streaming data visualization in many ways, but it can also help you to understand the status of a complex ecosystem. It's a good fit because it has information that you need to see and act on as soon as possible. It's also complex and needs to give you as much information as possible without trying to lead you to predetermined conclusions.

> It's not as important that the information presented is accurate as much as giving the person the idea that they need to make a decision.
>
> —Casey Rosenthal, manager at Netflix Chaos and Intuitive Engineering and one of the creators of Vizceral

Figure 5-3 shows an example of a streaming visualization. The open circles represent microservices. The connections between them in a process are the connecting lines. The dots on the lines represent traffic: an increase in volume is shown by more dots. This can quickly give someone an idea of the health and load of the system. The dots that represent traffic are not to scale, and they don't need to be in order to elicit an intuitive read by the observer.

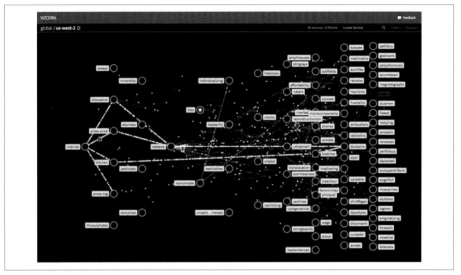

*Figure 5-3. A streaming visualization at Netflix (source: http://bit.ly/2LKKxkj)*

Processing for visualization and visualizing processing are both niches in much larger fields. Stream processing for visualizations is most likely going to be something new to you. Visualizing processing is helpful in understanding what's going on. Working together, these techniques can accomplish a lot.

# CHAPTER 6

# Developing a Client

 The workflow diagram at the beginning of the other chapters was intentionally left out of this one, as it doesn't have a place at the same level as the rest of the topics. The client is where the other subjects are applied. Which subjects are applied in the client (as opposed to other systems) depends on scale and complexity.

After you've identified and figured out how to process your streaming data, you need a way for people to be able to view and interact with it. The interface for presenting streaming data is known as a *client application*. The client can be in a browser, run on a device like a phone or desktop, or be firmware embedded in a device. In order to meet your needs for presenting streaming data in a useful manner, you may need to purpose-build a client for it.

One of the first things to consider is how much of the workload will be in the client. This choice is not as simple as delegating as much as possible to server components—the client will have a faster response time and be more interactive. Allowing the client to handle a portion of the load can also be significant for widely distributed applications. Anything that is consistent for all clients can be done on the server. Anything that needs to be customized per individual client makes sense to be done on the client.

We'll look at some of the other major considerations next, and go over the basics of creating a client application. There is one provided to help get you started quickly. You could also choose to apply the concepts introduced here to a different application or language if the provided client app isn't a starting point that works well for you.

# Native or Browser Development

A *native client* is one that is packaged for a specific device or operating system. You'll want to develop a native client when performance is your number one concern or you need to break out of the browser sandbox and interact with services on the system. Native clients also make sense when developing for a specific platform like an embedded device.

A *browser-based client* will be considerably easier to develop and for people to use. There is no install process, it's operating system–agnostic, and everyone has the prerequisites. There are some downsides too; for example, the browsers add overhead and some restrictions, and you are forced to use JavaScript as the language for logic. Still, developing a browser client is often a good choice. The power of most systems will easily compensate for the overhead, and performance should exceed the practical limits of what people are able to interpret.

Here's a breakdown of the main benefits of each approach:

| Browser client | Native client |
| --- | --- |
| No install, works everywhere | Higher performance |
| Common frameworks | More control |

It's also possible to get the best of both worlds by using a packager that allows you to bundle a web app with a browser and local libraries into a native app for Windows, macOS, and Linux. This application framework might not give you higher performance, but it will allow you to break some barriers that your browser cannot cross. Electron (*http://electron.atom.io/*) and nw.js (*https://nwjs.io/*) are both options that allow for writing native applications using web technologies. You can use the same code on a web server as you can in the packaged native client.

# Frameworks and Libraries

Once you've decided whether your client will be browser-based or native, you still have a lot of choices to make with respect to libraries and frameworks to help you get started. Two popular frameworks for a streaming client are AngularJS (by Google) and React (by Facebook). Both are great at presenting information immediately to the user with a minimal amount of development.

If you're developing a browser client, the biggest performance hit is HTML. Adding and removing elements from live HTML in the browser (aka the Document Object Model, or DOM) takes a lot of overhead, and you're also limited to what Cascading Style Sheets (CSS) allows for manipulating appearance. Scalable Vector Graphics (SVG) allows for unlimited flexibility in terms of appearance and manipulation but still carries with it the performance overhead of HTML. SVG is very capable, though, and is considered the current standard for data visualization in a browser. It's the primary renderer for popular libraries such as D3.js (*https://d3js.org/*). When SVG is not performant enough, WebGL (*https://en.wikipedia.org/wiki/WebGL*) is a good option. It has the flexibility and performance of a game engine, and can even use the hardware on graphics cards to help. The trade-off is that WebGL has a higher learning curve than the alternatives, and the libraries that have been built for it, such as three.js (*https://threejs.org/*), aren't as friendly. But with WebGL, the potential is unbounded. It even has libraries for augmented and virtual reality, which aren't really options for the others mentioned.

## A Common Approach

A common and recommended approach for developing a client is as follows. Consider this and adjust where needed:

- A browser client using Angular.js (*https://angularjs.org/*) or React.js (*https://facebook.github.io/react/*) is a good starting point.
- Use D3.js (*https://d3js.org/*) for typical visualizations where existing code can be easily applied.
- Use WebGL and a framework like three.js for any visualization that requires more complexity and performance.
- Categorize and organize the data into columns (see Chapter 11, *Streaming Data Dashboard*).
- Reduce the data volume and speed to something that can be easily interpreted.

Or start with the provided client app and keep building!

## Getting Started with the Sample Client Application

A simple starter app has been provided for you and is available on GitHub (*http://bit.ly/2LJwA6n*). The goal of the application is to get as much of the pesky boilerplate out of the way for you as possible so you can try things out quickly.

To get started with the sample app, you need only two things installed: Git and Node. Both are common and can run on Windows, macOS, and Linux. If you don't have these installed already, you will need to do so before proceeding. You'll be able to tell by any errors you get when trying to follow along.

First, clone the repo somewhere you can remember:

```
git clone https://github.com/SuddenDevelopment/Visualizing-Streaming-Data.git
```

Next, get all of the libraries, as shown in Example 6-1. The libraries are specified in the *packages.json* file.

*Example 6-1. Install all of the dependencies*

```
cd visualizing-streaming-data/client
```

```
npm install
```

ElectronForge and some of its dependencies may need to be installed globally and/or with some administrative privileges. This will take a while. If all goes well, you'll be able to start the client:

```
electron-forge start
```

If successful, you will get a screen that looks something like Figure 6-1.

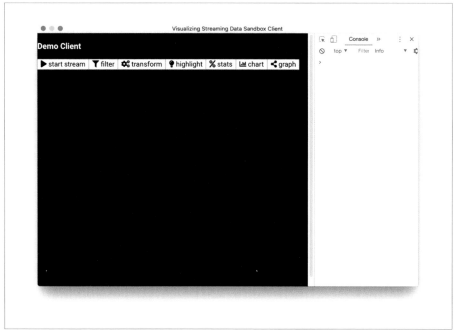

*Figure 6-1. Opening screen of demo client*

You can now build your app into an executable:

```
electron-forge build
```

# Client Libraries

The libraries used have been kept to a minimum. They were selected for simplicity over anything else. You can easily add libraries as you go, or trade out the ones used here. They are as follows:

*AngularJS 1.x (https://angularjs.org/)*

Angular is a framework that simplifies the tasks of adding listeners, building HTML, and connecting events. The result is an easy-to-understand framework that is ideal for prototyping. There are newer versions of Angular, but the 2.x versions jump in complexity; using an older version made it easier to convey the ideas in the book quickly.

*AngularJS Material (https://material.angularjs.org/latest/)*

Angular Material has a lot of predefined components and layouts and lets you put things together rapidly. This version of Material is specific to Angular, but every major framework has an implementation of Material principles and components. You can also find standalone Material implementations.

*Electron (https://electronjs.org/)*

Electron is a project that will wrap your code, Node.js, and Chrome into an executable package. This combination creates a large package (80 MB+) but allows you to use your web development skills to create native applications. There are a few things that browsers can't do for security reasons. Electron allows you to bypass those barriers.

*Electron Forge (https://electronforge.io/)*

Electron Forge gathers all of the most commonly needed Electron projects into an easy-to-use framework. All of the functionality of the underlying packages for building executables and installers is there, and you can supply them as options to Electron Forge. Eventually, your skills in building Electron packages may go beyond Electron Forge, but until then it's a great place to start.

*Faker (https://github.com/marak/Faker.js/)*

Faker is a useful library for generating test data. It can be used to quickly mock up applications with realistic data. For the demo client, I generate a record with data from this library every second.

*Font Awesome (https://fontawesome.com/)*

Font Awesome isn't as necessary as the other libraries, but it's hard to imagine creating a presentation without it. Font Awesome is an icon library that has thousands of SVG icons in a CSS framework that is easy to use and manipulate.

# Code Structure

The example client files are as simple as possible given the libraries used. You can make the client as complex as you like for your organization's needs, as long as you modify the paths that point to the files in the code. The current structure is as follows:

```
client/
  src/
    index.js --Electron main app file
    index.html --Primary web page
    index.css --Primary stylesheet
    app.js --Primary JavaScript
    partials/ --Angular snippet files to be included
      chart.htm
      json.htm
      stats.htm
```

The demo app has functionality divided by buttons. The buttons allow you to see the impact of your changes to the code separately. This isn't typical for an application. This organization is to make it easier to understand how to edit the code. Clicking each button toggles its "enabled" state. For example, pressing the Filter button runs the filtering function in *app.js*:

```
if($scope.objButtons.filter.enabled===true){
    // modify object, null if it shouldn't be shown at all
    $scope.fnFilter(objMsg);
}
```

To start with, a new record is created every second with fake data from Faker. You will want to change the contents of this function to connect to your streaming source:

```
$scope.fnStartStream=function(){
    $scope.title='Streaming'
    var objStream=setInterval(function(){
        var objMsg={
            "user":libBS.internet.userName(),
            "ip": libBS.internet.ip(),
            "agent": libBS.internet.userAgent(),
            "job": libBS.name.jobType()
        };
        $scope.fnOnMessage(objMsg);
    }, 1000);
};
```

You should keep the reference to the `fnOnMessage` function, but call it every time you get a message instead of every second. As your code matures, `fnOnMessage` will be the function that controls the other actions the client is set up for. It will put data into collections, get the statistics, format the data for visualizations, kick off downstream events, and be one of the tickers in the application you can use to gauge decisions. A basic example of this function might look like this:

```
$scope.fnOnMessage=function(objMsg){
    if($scope.objButtons.filter.enabled===true){
        $scope.fnFilter(objMsg);
    }
    if(objMsg !== null){
        $scope.arrData.unshift(objMsg);
    }
```

```
    $scope.$evalAsync();
    };
```

The partial files are shown when needed. Separating functional example components of the client into their own files cuts down on a lot of clutter, but otherwise
is not necessary. You can include them dynamically with code like the following:

```
<div ng-if="objButtons.chart.enabled===true"
     ng-include="'./partials/chart.htm'" flex></div>
```

I hope this gives you an easy starting point for trying out various techniques in
this book. Many of the earlier topics we covered, such as processing, can be done
in the client as well if the data volume is below a certain level.

# Alternative Approaches

You may want to change the client approach right away. Here are a few alternatives that might make sense:

http-server *(https://www.npmjs.com/package/http-server)*
> If you don't want to mess with Electron at all, you can set up a simple web
> server. This is the simplest one I have found; it's great for testing and devel-
> oping. Simply run the client in a browser with http-server and then go to
> *http://localhost:8080*:

```
            http-server ./client/
```

*React (https://reactjs.org/)*
> React is a popular framework that is similar to Angular. It may make sense if
> your organization has standardized on React or you know you like the way
> it's structured.

*Vue.js (https://vuejs.org/)*
> Vue.js was inspired by Angular 1.x and has a lot of similarities to it. It's not as
> popular as React but sits somewhere between React and Angular in terms of
> complexity versus speed.

If you are excited at all about doing something interactive and/or visual with
streaming data, I highly encourage you to create a client to test things out. So
many things sound like they make sense until you go to apply them and discover
what's missing!

# CHAPTER 7

# Presenting Streaming Data

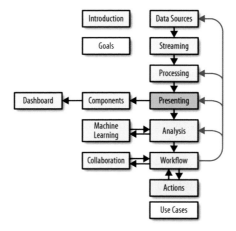

This chapter introduces some topics and elements to consider with regard to presentation. It can be used like an idea generator that you revisit as needed to see if any of the mentioned elements make sense to incorporate.

Staring at thousands or millions of raw records is not very efficient or sustainable for any goal. It's important to know what the raw data looks like, but only in order to understand what would be interesting to summarize in a more friendly format. Visualizations are that friendlier format. They engage a different part of the brain that understands color, spatial references, and patterns. Visualizations have such an immediate impact on the viewer that they are often used to imply a conclusion from data. This is why there is a natural division in data visualization goals among sales, reporting, and analysis.

Visualizations can be employed to more effectively achieve all of these goals. They can take overwhelming amounts of information and present it in a way that can be easily understood. A "sparkline" can show a pattern of values over time, including the minimum, maximum, average, first, and last values, all within a space that is typically reserved for just a couple of values. This represents a huge increase in data density. Visualizations can also be used to tap into a common lexicon of meaningful images and styles. Translating text into recognizable icons can increase the consumable data density without any explanation needed. A common use of this is displaying male and female icons when showing statistics for demographics. Of course, there is always a proportional trade-off between gaining data density and losing context and nuance. The higher the data density, the more patterns, anomalies, and unasked questions will be abstracted away. This is why the various levels of visualizations work well in an iterative process.

# Showing Streaming Data

All streaming data can be presented. Streaming records to the console as they are generated is the original streaming data visualization. In a streaming data client, you can apply a lot of enhancements to that. It's definitely recommended to stream some data in the client as opposed to having only stats and visualizations, to provide context and supporting evidence. The records can be organized in various ways and then have visual cues and styles added to them to help the viewer understand what is flying by and how it relates to everything else being presented.

Figure 7-1 is a modern approach that emulates streaming data in a console so that it can add some functionality that a console cannot do.

*Figure 7-1. Example from log.io of streaming records in a client*

# Events

*Event-based data* is what we call data that is the result of something occurring. This data is not simply polled or collected or queried. Events naturally fit well into streaming data visualizations because the time when they occur in relation to each other can have meaning and show prominently. Some technical considerations of streaming event-based data are as follows:

- Events can be acted upon immediately only up to a performance threshold, where they start to get backlogged. At this point, you need to batch, trim, or distribute the workload.

- If a timestamp is not already added to the events, create one. If there are several steps in the lifetime of an event, keep a separate timestamp for each; they can be significant when distinct. You can always keep a last_updated timestamp additionally if needed.

- If you treat all events as batches within time limits, you will save yourself some headaches.

Showing the differences in data as they occur works only up to a certain threshold. Once that is greater than one change per second, too much overhead is required to visually update the information, and anyone watching it can't absorb it. To avoid those issues, you can keep batches of data to process every second and update the display. Example 7-1 shows how this works.

*Example 7-1. Batch everything in a time frame, and then process*

```
// a time reference is needed to keep track of batches
var intBatchStartTime=Date.now();
// an array to hold the batches
var arrBatch=[];
// a function to be called on events
var fnOnEvent=function(objEvent){
  var intNow=Date.now();
  // always add the event to the batch
  arrBatch.push(objEvent);
  if(intBatchStartTime+1000<intNow){
    // time to process call the function that processes
    // note that if the array isn't copied, it will have a race condition
    fnProcessBatch(arrBatch);
    // reset the batch
    arrBatch=[];
    intBatchStartTime=intNow;
  }
}
```

# Logs

*Logs* are records of events that are commonly saved to a file. By far the most common streaming data watched is updates to a log file in a console. This is typically done with the Unix command `tail -f <filename>`. You can do this with error logs and watch the servers, behind-the-scenes reactions to your interactions. The console is pretty limited, though. It can be hard to pick out significant information or do anything with it. In order to have more options, you can bring the same log files into a streaming data client with a library like `node-tail` (*http://bit.ly/2sqn5Ai*). Example 7-2 illustrates its use.

*Example 7-2. Tailing a log file with node-tail*

```
// watch a file
tail = new Tail("fileToTail");
// fire every time a new line comes in
tail.on("line", function(strLine) {
  // call your defined function for the event
  // note: in most cases you'll need to parse the string
  fnOnEvent(strLine);
});
```

# Records

*Records* are what is returned when querying a database. In most cases, the records need to be seen all at once and in a grid ordered on significant fields that aren't chronological. This is a good fit for a streaming visualization only if the records have timestamps and if there's some value in showing them chronologically. For example, streaming records at an interval can be used as a playback of events from a point in time. When working with records, you are completely outside an event-based pattern. You can either show a number of records per second or play them back as events with a relative or accelerated time scale. Example 7-3 shows how to stream a record per `intDelay`, where `intDelay` is in milliseconds.

*Example 7-3. Records per second*

```
// use set interval for timing, this var will be a reference to it
var objThrottle={};
// assuming arrRecords is a collection of records
objThrottle=setInterval(function(){
  // assuming fnSendRecord is the function to run for each record
  fnSendRecord(arrRecords[intIndex]);
  if(intIndex===intRecords-1){ clearInterval(objThrottle); }
  else{ intIndex++; }
}, intDelay);
```

# Dashboards

A streaming data dashboard will bring together several elements that share context. A typical dashboard has some common rules. According to *Information Dashboard Design* by Stephen Few (O'Reilly), it should provide information at a glance and be displayed on a single page. Figure 7-2 shows an example of such a dashboard.

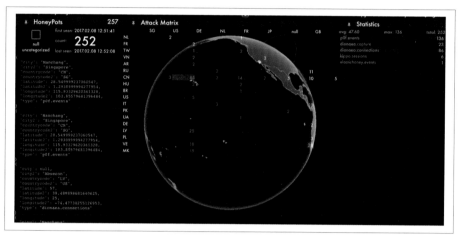

*Figure 7-2. Multiple elements in a streaming data dashboard (source: https://ohm.ai)*

We will go over the options for assembling a streaming data dashboard in Chapter 11. For now, it's good to keep this end goal in mind while reviewing the elements that will compose it.

# Visual Elements and Properties

A lot of visual elements and properties can be used in visualizations. The choice can be daunting. The following list shows some examples of when using them makes good sense. All of the examples can be found in the file *elements.htm* in the accompanying code repository.

## Containers

A container is a grouping of elements with a border. The border doesn't need to be a line; it can also be spacing. Containers can take many shapes that have their own terms.

**When to use it:**

When a distinct separation between groups of items is needed.

| Container 1 | Container 2 |
|:---:|:---:|
| Record | Record |
| Record | Record |
| Record | Record |
| Record | Record |

## Visibility

Elements can be hidden, shown, or have varying levels of transparency.

**When to use it:**

Show what's significant at the time and hide what is not. Use transparency to give a vague idea of what's going on behind.

**Tip:**

Use the CSS opacity property for transparency.

| Container 1 | Container 2 |
|:---:|:---:|
| Record | Record |
| Record | Record |
| Record | Record |
| Record | Record |

## Color

Color can be modified on nearly all elements to represent something significant. Color requires some thought and consistency across elements to be most effective.

**When to use it:**

Only when the color has consistent meaning.

| Container 1 | Container 2 |
| --- | --- |
| Info | Good |
| Warn | Complete |
| Alarm | Unknown |
| Highlight | Info |

## Background

Background fills can be used as an indicator for the entire record that stands out. A select few background colors should be chosen, ensuring that the overlying text and elements are still readable.

**When to use it:**

As a quick reference of meaning for the record as a whole, conveying status, priority, significance, or type.

```
{
  "place": {
    "country_code": "BR"
  },
  "text": "Relendo estes RPGs que estavam pe
}

{
  "place": {
    "country_code": "PH"
  },
  "text": "@kittyhalei24 ahahahahahhahaah gr
}

{
  "place": {
    "country_code": "US"
  },
  "text": "õŸ˜ª https://t.co/sRqjsoH6GV"
}

{
  "place": {
    "country_code": "VE"
  },
  "text": "Yo te quiero tener"
}
```

## Size

Size is an intuitive indicator of weight, importance, priority, or volume. Too much size variance can make things too difficult to read. Best practice is to use a few predefined sizes that have meaning.

**When to use it:**

To convey a higher or lower weight than normal. Use as an exception.

```
"place":
  "country_code": "BR"

"text": "Relendo estes RPGs que estavam pe

"place":
  "country code": "PH"

"text": "@kittyhalei24 ahahahahahhahaah grabe ka hard!"

{
  "place": {
    "country_code": "US"
  },
  "text": "ðŸ˜ª https://t.co/:
}

"place":
  "country code": "VE"

"text": "Yo te quiero tener"
```

## Borders

Outlines of a container that can vary in shape, style, color, thickness, and opacity.

**When to use it:**

To clearly and quickly show a state for everything within a container.

**Tip:**

Use CSS `border` and `border-radius` styles.

```
"place":
  "country_code": "BR"

"text": "Relendo estes RPGs que estavam pe

"place":
  "country_code": "PH"

"text": "@kittyhalei24 ahahahahahhahaah gi

"place":
  "country_code": "US"

"text": "ðŸ˜ª https://t.co/sRqjsoH6GV"

"place":
  "country_code": "VE"

"text": "Yo te quiero tener"
```

## Alignment

Also known as *justification*. Alignment refers to the placement of elements and use of negative space within a container.

**When to use it:**

Use sparingly when the intuitive effect is beneficial, such as right-aligning numbers while text is left-aligned.

## Fonts

Fonts are a passionate subject in design. They can have a powerful impact, so when they are abused or unwittingly misused, it can be a big detractor. When used cautiously, deliberately, and with purpose, they can be a useful detail.

**When to use it:**

Syntax highlighting, title versus body, key versus value, label versus input (not all of these at once).

**Tip**:

Google Fonts (*https://fonts.google.com/*) is a great place to start.

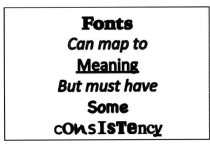

*Layout*

Layouts help create a logical flow of items that are shown.

**When to use it:**

When more than one set of elements is presented.

**Tip:**

Use CSS Flexbox (*http://bit.ly/2L8bihB*).

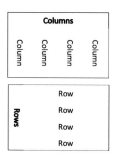

*Thickness*

Thickness can intuitively translate to weight or volume. Borders, connecting lines, dividing lines, edges, and other elements can have thickness mapped to a meaningful value.

**When to use it:**

To convey weight or volume.

**Tip**:

Use the CSS `border` properties.

```
"place":
  "country_code": "BR"

"text": "Relendo estes RPGs que estavam pe


"place":
  "country_code": "PH"

"text": "@kittyhalei24 ahahahahahhahaah g


"place":
  "country_code": "US"

"text": "ðŸ˜ https://t.co/sRqjsoH6GV"


"place":
  "country_code": "VE"

"text": "Yo te quiero tener"
```

## Spacing

Spacing can hold meaning but is more commonly used as something necessary for readability. It's used in code to show hierarchy and is used in data
formats as well.

**When to use it:**

For readability.

**Tip**:

Use the CSS `padding` and `margin` properties.

```
"place": {
    "country_code": "BR"

"text": "Relendo estes RPGs que estavam pe
```

```
"place": {
    "country_code": "PH"

"text": "@kittyhalei24 ahahahahahhahaah q:
```

```
"place": {
    "country_code": "US"

"text": "ÒŸ˜ https://t.co/sRqjsoH6GV"
```

```
"place": {
    "country_code": "VE"

"text": "Yo te quiero tener"
```

## Adjacency

*Adjacency* refers to elements being next to each other. This happens naturally, but carries intuitive meaning. When you use this feature intentionally,
you can take advantage of this intuitive meaning.

**When to use it:**

Use adjacency when a relationship (or lack thereof) is relevant.

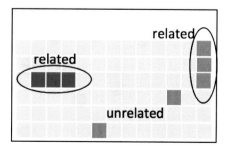

*Position*

Element positions easily translate to their relationships with all of the other elements, indicating what's related, what's new and old, and what's in between.

**When to use it:**

Always. The elements will all end up somewhere, so put them somewhere deliberately.

**Tip**:

Use the CSS top, bottom, left, right, float, and position properties.

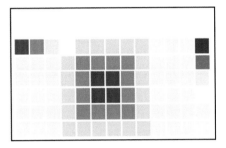

*Connections, relationships*

Connections are used to show relationships between elements. The connections can have meaning mapped to thickness, color, labels, and direction. This example was found at *http://js.cytoscape.org/*.

**When to use it:**

To indicate relationships.

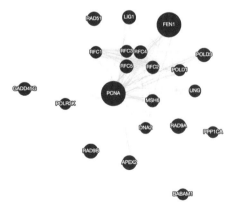

*Images*

Images provided as content as well as images created based on content can add a lot of information quickly. They can also quickly take up a lot of precious screen real estate, so show them when they might be of most benefit and crop them to the most information-rich portion if possible.

**When to use it:**

When images are the subject of the record or an image can be used for a quick intuitive decision, like with a screenshot of a website.

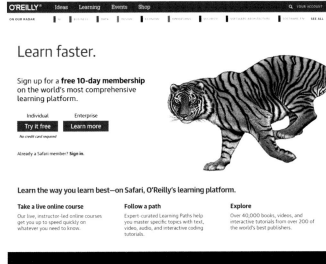

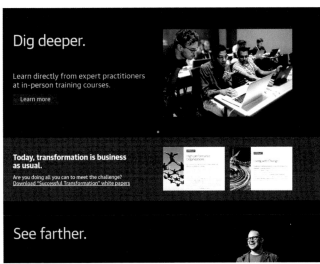

*Icons*

Icons are especially useful for things like tags, where they can consistently represent common elements.

**When to use it:**

When you have something that can frequently and consistently be represented by an icon that is useful as a fast visual cue.

**Tip**:

Use Font Awesome (*http://fontawesome.io/*).

icons

```
{
  "place": {
    "country_code": "BR"
  },
  "_tags": [
    "bell"
  ],
  "text": "Relendo estes RPGs qu
} 🔔

{
  "place": {
    "country_code": "PH"
  },
  "_tags": [
    "bomb"
  ],
  "text": "@kittyhalei24 ahahaha
} 💣

{
  "place": {
    "country_code": "US"
  },
  "_tags": [
    "bug"
  ],
  "text": "ðŸ˜ª https://t.co/sRc
} 🐛
```

*Shape*

The shape of an element is usually a consistent style choice. A deliberate attempt at making something look edgy might have nonsquare corners. This doesn't mean shape can't be used effectively to convey meaning; that meaning is just less likely to be intuitive.

**When to use it:**

As a record-level indicator of something like status or type.

**Tip**:

Use the CSS `border-radius` property.

```
"place":
    "country_code": "BR"

"text": "Relendo estes RPGs que estavam pe

"place":
    "country_code": "PH"

"text": "@kittyhalei24 ahahahahahhahaah g:

"place":
    "country_code": "US"

"text": "óÿ'ø https://t.co/sRqjsoH6GV"

"place":
    "country_code": "VE"

"text": "Yo te quiero tener"
```

## *Movement*

Movement draws a lot of attention initially. After that, there needs to be an instant and clear reason to keep the viewer's attention. Almost everything can be moving at once as long as the movement has a pattern and purpose that can be intuitively understood. Movements can be between positions or within an existing position (shake).

**When to use it:**

For transitions and updates.

**Tip**:

Use CSS animations (*http://bit.ly/2shABHg*) and transitions, and/or SVG animations (*http://bit.ly/2kyvhLg*).

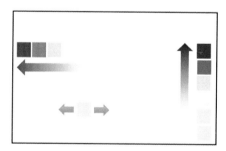

# Data Density

An overall characteristic of the visual elements, used in combination, is data density. *Data density* refers to the number of useful data points you can get into an area. Streaming data usually comes with the challenge of how to see more information at once. Considering the data density can make a big impact on the effectiveness of what you are visualizing. The higher the data density, the larger the scope. As data density increases, the amount of data shown per record will decrease; a line chart can represent any number of data points and allow zooming, but allows mapping only one quantifiable metric per line. The inverse is also true. The more data you show per record, the fewer records you can represent (Table 7-1). Be mindful of the amount of negative space that is left when working towards greater data density. If the information can't be interpreted, then it doesn't count. Information that is hidden under layers of overlapping elements doesn't count towards data density. Similarly, if there is so much information in a visualization that elements cannot be distinguished from one another, their relationships and positions will not convey anything meaningful.

*Table 7-1. Data density*

|  | Records | Points per record | Cues |
|---|---|---|---|
| **Console 1 line per record** | 80 | Up to ~12 | Color, font |
| **Console syntax expanded** | 1–25 | All | Color, font, icons, styles |
| **Dynamic icons** | 800 | ~10 | Color, shape, icons, order |
| **Icons** | 3,000 | 2 | Color, icon, order |
| **Chart** | Resolution-bound | 1 per series | Color, order |

# Dividing Time

Because of the nature of a visualization that is always updating, it's necessary to include some time references so that viewers can tell the difference between new items and old (on anything besides a chart including time as an axis). A few ways of doing this are as follows:

- Divide by moving windows with "now" as a reference point.
- Divide by occurring time such as yesterday, the previous hour, and this hour, crossing thresholds.
- Show what is about to leave the cache and what is new.
- Use significant events as markers for "before" and "after."

Figures 7-3 through 7-5 show examples of what these strategies might look like.

*Figure 7-3. Dividing time by time increments (methods #1 and #2)*

*Figure 7-4. Dividing records by buffer location (method #3)*

*Figure 7-5. Event-based time dividers (method #4)*

The intent of the visualization should help you decide which one to use. If everything is in reference to now, without any concern for natural time or events, then show everything in referential time. This can fit well when a queue is time-based —if you are in a support center, it's more important to know that an issue is 2 hours old than that it occurred at 2 p.m. FThere is an excellent open source library that can help make these time conversions called Moment.js (*https:// momentjs.com/*). It perfectly fits the common need of converting between representations of time:

```
moment().subtract(10, 'days').calendar(); // 02/07/2017
moment("20111031", "YYYYMMDD").fromNow(); // 5 years ago
moment().format('MMMM Do YYYY'); // February 17th 2017
```

Because of the way JavaScript links everything, it can be difficult to keep a predictable window on a position within an array that is always changing. To simplify this, I use a library called Immutable.js (*https://facebook.github.io/ immutable-js/*). Example 7-4 illustrates its use.

*Example 7-4. Using Immutable.js instead of arrays for buffers*

```
// create an Immutable list instead of an array
arrCache = Immutable.List();
// add to it as new events come in
arrCache = arrCache.concat(arrData);
// set the window you want, start and finish
var arrWindow=arrCache.slice(0,100);
```

Events are an especially impactful way to organize records, but this is an often overlooked context. If you are aware of the events that have a contextual impact on the records before and after them, use include records bracketing the current event when possible. Dividing records by events will require some extra work in creating a legend because each event will need to look different in order to be distinguished. The legend should have a representation of the elements used for the events as well as the time frame of the events in order of occurrence.

It's possible to implement multiple techniques at once, but it can get complex quickly. Whatever strategy is employed, a legend to explain it will be useful.

# Time to Live

In addition to having time windows, you will also need to display some things that are more persistent but time out after a while. This is significant in a streaming visualization where you don't have a hard limit on the number of items displayed. You need some way to avoid them piling up cumulatively. It helps if you can make the timeouts based on context—something of higher severity needs to stay visible longer than something that is informational.

Examples 7-5 and 7-6 demonstrate setting a time to live on an object and timing out an object.

*Example 7-5. Setting a time to live*

```
// assume objMsg is already defined
// in this scenario a severity property is already present as a number
if(typeof objMsg.severity === 'number'){
  // need a timestamp as a point of reference
  objMsg.timestamp=Date.now();
  // ttl is set in milliseconds
    objMsg.ttl=objMsg.severity*60000;
}
```

*Example 7-6. Timing out*

```
// run inside a function that scans all persistent objects
// get the current timestamp
var intNow = Date.now();
// arrObjects as a collection of objects
for(var i=0;i<arrobjects.length;i++){
 if(arrObjects[i].timestamp+arrObjects[i].ttl < intNow){
   // this is past the timeout threshold
   // call whatever function is defined to remove the timed-out object
   fnRemove(arrObjects[i]);
 }
}
```

Time to live doesn't need to be a binary thing. It can also allow for a change of state—for example, you might allow a warning to become an information item after a few minutes. Changing state can feel a lot more dynamic. Each state can have a different time to live and display properties, and items end up having stages of being displayed. Example 7-7 demonstrates how this might work.

*Example 7-7. Time in state*

```
// run inside a function that scans all persistent objects
// get the current timestamp
var intNow = Date.now();
// arrObjects as a collection of objects
for(var i=0;i<arrobjects.length;i++){
if(arrObjects[i].timestamp+arrObjects[i].ttl < intNow){
   // this is past the timeout threshold
   // call whatever function is defined to remove the timed-out object
   if(arrObjects[i].severity > 0)
   {
     // reduce the severity and recalc the ttl
     arrObjects[i].severity--;
     arrObjects[i].ttl=objMsg.severity*60000;
   }else{
     fnRemove(arrObjects[i]);
   }
 }
}
```

# Context

Context is critical for visualizations of any type. Any data that exists in a context related to other information needs to be presented in context. Isolating data will not just remove context; it will create a new and misleading context.

Streaming data has a natural context of time, but other contexts can be just as important and need to be deliberately considered for their utility. Here are some contextual questions to keep in mind when planning your presentation:

- When did a record occur?
- When did it occur in relation to another event?
- Is this occurrence common?
- How do the numeric values compare to others?
- How often do the text values occur?
- Is this unusual in any way?
- Is there enough information to make a meaningful comparison?

An example of the importance of context can be found in the honeypot data collected by threat intelligence companies like Norse to report on worldwide cyberattacks. *Honeypots* are devices set up to be targets for malicious activity that is recorded and monitored. A streaming data visualization of that activity can warn you of any attacks on the decoy that is meant to appear as what you are trying to protect. Watching a site set up for this purpose might lead you to some hasty conclusions, such as the following:

- "China is attacking everyone!"
- "The United States is attacking everyone!"
- "Everyone with a computer is attacking everyone!"
- "<Insert_recognizable_company_name> is really aggressive!"

But several levels of context are missing that would become apparent over time or with industry experience. Here are a few points to consider:

- Calling all of this activity an "attack" can be misleading. Most of it is the result of wide internet scans of services, which could be interpreted as reconnaissance for a later attack but is not really an attack in itself.
- This activity is always occurring, and from everywhere that has internet access. The more connected a region is, the more of this activity occurs.
- Attacks are not country-specific. The IP addresses seen by honeypots are, but the people behind such activity are often not in the same location as the identified machines. Some of them are compromised machines, or the activity may have several hops and only the last one is visible.
- The listed names are only of the known owners of those machines seen by the honeypots.
- What might have attracted activity to a particular honeypot, if anything, is not shown.
- The difference between current and past activity is not shown.

The streaming data visualization shown in Figure 7-6 was a great success in its intended purpose of publicity but is an equally good example of missing critical context. The site inspired several people to be cybersleuths and watch it for patterns that would explain outages and hacks.

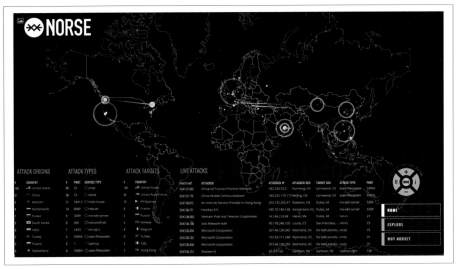

*Figure 7-6. The Live Norse Attack Map (http://map.norsecorp.com/)*

# Visual Language

Companies and products establish *visual languages,* also known as design systems or visual design systems, for many reasons. A consistent and unified visual language can make your product more rapidly expandable (you can reuse and leverage), it can make it easier for users to understand the product—with consistent affordances for all the controls (shallow learning curve, less training, fewer errors, faster completion time per task, etc.). A visual language can communicate the brand messaging of a product or firm by visually informing users what they stand for. A sophisticated visual language is often connected to design principles, which are core statements that guide the decision making of what a product should do and how it should be designed. A thoughtful design system makes a product easier to understand and use. As Kaari Saarinen, Design Language System lead at Airbnb, puts it (*http://bit.ly/2LKBgZV*):

> Our designs should be unified platforms that drive greater efficiency through well-defined and reusable components...A unified design language shouldn't be just a set of static rules and individual atoms; it should be an evolving ecosystem.

The guiding principles at Airbnb are that the designs should be unified, universal, iconic, and conversational.

Figure 7-7 is a description of the visual language developed for the SpringRain streaming network visualization. It shows a lot of thought given to all of the visual elements that can be mapped to give someone an intuitive understanding of what's going on when they happen to look at it. The overall effect feels natural in its movement: new things come in at the top, trickle down, accumulate, and settle into history at the bottom (see Figure 7-8). This movement has meaning without being overwhelming.

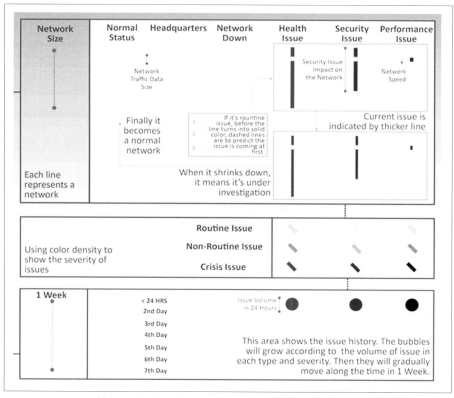

*Figure 7-7. Visual language developed for a streaming network visualization (source: http://bit.ly/2IV37bQ)*

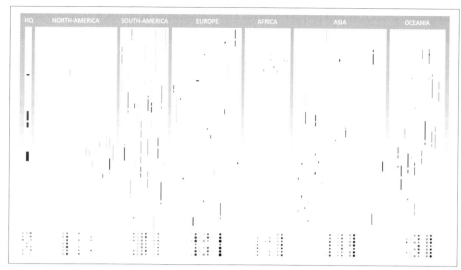

*Figure 7-8. The SpringRain streaming network data visualization (source: http://bit.ly/2IUuqmJ)*

# Appropriate Displays

When presenting streaming data, the likelihood is high that there will be a lot more data than can be shown. Consider how it will be organized and navigated. Allow different levels of focus and view.

You'll also need to consider the devices your data presentation will be viewed on, or the devices you will need to develop toward. Their resolution, distribution, and mode of interaction can have a big impact on the direction you need to take with designing and implementing an interface.

Standard 1080p HD displays have 1920 × 1080 pixels. The pixels get rather distinct at larger screen sizes. This can be a considered the lowest common denominator of desktop displays. You can safely assume this is the resolution of a ~15-inch diagonal screen if you are developing for desktops and laptops.

4K screens have four times the resolution of 1080p displays and are often used with high-end desktops and laptops for which fine resolution is appreciated and can be afforded. There are higher-resolution standards as well, but the higher resolutions won't have as much impact on your decisions as the screen sizes. A 4K screen is most commonly found in a living room, meeting room, or showroom floor. They are great for passive presentations, or displaying multiple views at once.

Phone resolutions are increasing, but the sizes remain relatively small. The resolution is typically similar to 1080p, but in a ~5-inch diagonal screen. This form factor will limit the scope of data that can be seen at once. You can still design for these devices, but it will require giving a lot of thought to what is seen when and how to navigate between focused views.

Tablets have a wide range of screen sizes. It's difficult to accommodate them all based on size and resolution. They have larger screens than phones but, like phones, are touch-interactive. The touch interaction is the most significant feature that can be used on these displays. If supporting tablets, consider building in support for typical touch gestures.

When displays are beyond a certain size—say, ~65 inches diagonal—they might as well be considered walls or installations. These displays tend to be more casual and ambient. They either exist at an atmospheric awareness level, or are something you might play with in passing (see Figure 7-9).

*Figure 7-9. Interactive wall at Google in NY (source: https://googlecreative-lab.github.io/anypixel/)*

Virtual reality (*https://en.wikipedia.org/wiki/Virtual_reality*) environments are interesting. There aren't a lot of explorations into practical data visualization within them. They typically either have the equivalent of a wall display or offer some way to explore in 3D (see Figure 7-10). One of the significant limitations of these displays is that they limit the ability to share the experience with anyone who doesn't also have a VR device. This is certainly an area to explore in the future.

> Practical VR use is 2–5 years away; we are in a prototyping phase now.
>
> —Weidong Yang, CEO at Kineviz (*http://kineviz.com*)

*Figure 7-10. Weidong, from Kineviz, guiding someone through a VR data visualization*

Augmented reality (*https://en.wikipedia.org/wiki/Augmented_reality*) uses a device to allow you to map virtual visuals as if they were in the real world. There's definitely an application for streaming data to be visualized over the real-world objects it's related to. One of the most promising aspects of this concept and technology is the potential for it to break out of the form factors and their limitations mentioned previously.

This chapter covered a lot of ground. It's meant to be a resource to spark ideas more than a recipe to follow. Presenting streaming data is pretty immature, and there aren't a lot of rules. Question any rules that are intended for static presentations. Try them out and see how they apply to streaming data visualizations.

# CHAPTER 8

# Visualization Components

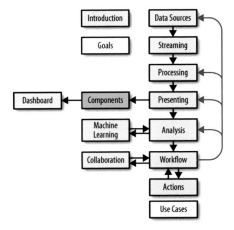

*Components* are the discrete blocks of applied elements that are used in visualizations. This chapter covers some common visualization components with a streaming data update.

## Records

By the time records are being shown to an analyst, they should have some level of structure applied to them, using the methods mentioned in Chapter 5. The more structure is applied to them, the easier it will be to organize and create rules about them.

At some point in a streaming data client, you will need to display raw records and allow someone to add context or make decisions about them. This can be challenging when you have way more records than can ever be interpreted by one person, and each one may take an entire screen to display. The goals are typically as follows:

- Show as many records as possible to the analyst at once.
- Format the records in a readable way.
- Show the analyst only information that is relevant to what they are trying to accomplish.
- Add visual cues to records that help the analyst quickly notice significant details.
- Manage the speed of the data so that they can digest it.

Figure 8-1 shows an example of a record with such visual cues.

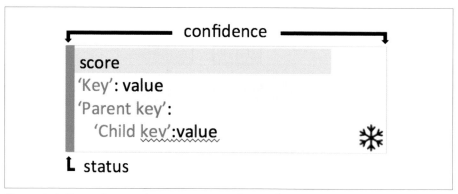

*Figure 8-1. Example record presentation with visual cues*

We can accomplish these goals with the following techniques:

- Use the processing techniques mentioned in Chapter 5.
- Visually format the record in the client—highlight syntax, distinguish between keys and values, etc.
- Add icons for tags, styles for categories, and other meaningful elements mentioned in the previous chapter.
- Buffer the data so that it can be streamed to the analyst at a speed they can handle and adjust (see Chapter 4).

# Statistics

> There are lies, damn lies, and statistics.
>
> —Mark Twain

Mark Twain's famous quote refers to the persuasive power of statistics. If you already knew the outcome, you could use statistics in this way with streaming data, but this is not usually the case when presenting such data. Presenting streaming data is not well suited to the goal of convincing someone of a predetermined conclusion. Statistics give the viewer a larger context to understand what they are seeing. If you see an item and it has a category associated with it, it helps to know how frequently that category shows up. When you see a score or anything quantitative, it can be helpful to know where it fits in the range of values seen within different time frames—it might be the highest value seen in the current hour but average in a 24-hour window.

The following general statistics are easy to make accessible, if not always visible, and can be added to any display of streaming data:

*Range*
> The minimum and maximum define a range of current values. Knowing the range can help understand where values fall within it.

*Average and quartiles*
> These smaller ranges help to quickly categorize the data within the larger range. It can be useful to group values into these subranges instead of making all decisions based on their more granular positions within the larger range. For example, it might be useful to know if a value is above the 75% threshold of the values seen.

*Value counts*
> Values that aren't quantitative need to be counted before numeric statistics can be applied to them.

*Intersection of values*
> How many times did two values coincide? This holds extra significance over counting them individually. If person 1 is the top attacker and person 2 is the top defender, you can't assume that person 1 is the top attacker of person 2 without counting the number of times they intersected.

*Bucket counts*
> When there are a lot of unique values, numerical or not, it can help to group them and add their values. Keep the ungrouped values for a more focused drill-down later, but this grouping can help make things easier to digest. For example, there are a lot of different types of messages you can get from logs. Getting them all as individual codes can be overwhelming. You can group them into application, error, info, and security events to get a high-level view.

Example 8-1 shows how you can collect several simple statistics by using a single function that is run for each record. When streaming, this is an efficient way to get this data. It keeps you from needing to loop through a collection of data for each statistic.

*Example 8-1. Keeping simple streaming stats*

```
var intMin=null, intMax=null, intTotal=0, intCount=0;
var objUniqueValues={};
var fnOnMessage=function(objMsg){
  // assuming objMsg.value is a number
  if(objMsg.value > intMax || intMax===null){
    intMax=objMsg.value;
  }
  if(objMsg.value < intMin || intMin===null){
    intMin=objMsg.value;
  }
  intTotal+=objMsg.value;
  intCount++;
  if(typeof objUniqueValues[objMsg.value] === 'undefined'){
    objUniqueValues[objMsg.value]=1;
  }else{
    objUniqueValues[objMsg.value]=++;
  }
}
```

Tracking and showing the cumulative statistics is useful, but this approach suffers from being transitory and hides what happened in smaller time windows. If you have a burst of errors every day in the same 5 minutes, you don't want it to get washed out in a 24-hour window; you should see a burst in the corresponding time window that stands out. In order to achieve this, consider the following:

- Choose a time window that makes sense for you for example, hourly as a default view.
- Keep statistics at smaller increments if possible—it's easy to make larger time window statistics from smaller ones.
- Allow quick comparisons between statistics windows.
- Allow several views of small multiples (*http://bit.ly/2kBUEvO*) to show multiple time frames at once and compare them visually.

Example 8-2 shows the process of keeping small time windows as separate stats and then using those stats to create the larger ones. If you have stats for every minute, creating the hourly stats from those instead of from the records is a lot more efficient, even if it takes more effort. When it comes to streaming data at high volumes, working with small time windows may be the only option to do it fast enough.

*Example 8-2. Keeping track of time windows*

```javascript
var updateWindows = function(arrData, objStat){
  // console.log(arrData,objStat);
  // does a new bucket need to be created?
  // var intNow=Date.now(); // shouldn't be needed, can use ls
  if(objStat.windows.current.fs < objStat.ls-60000 ){
    // take current bucket, snapshot it to history
    objStat.windows.minute.push(objStat.windows.current);
    // re-init current bucket
    objStat.windows.current =
      _.defaults({},objDefaults[objStat.type]());
    if(objStat.windows.hasOwnProperty('hour')
      && objStat.windows.ts_hour < objStat.ls-360000){
      // loop through minutes and drop off anything older than an hour
      objStat.windows.minute =
        _.filterOld(objStat.windows.minute, 'fs', 360000);
      // then take the remaining ones to aggregate into an hour
      objStat.windows.hour.push(
        aggStats[objStat.type](objStat.windows.minute)
      );
      objStat.windows.ts_hour = objStat.ls;
    }
    if(objStat.windows.hasOwnProperty('day')
      && objStat.windows.ts_hour < objStat.ls-86400000){
      // loop through minutes and drop off anything older than an hour
      objStat.windows.hour =
        _.filterOld(objStat.windows.hour, 'fs', 86400000);
      // then take the remaining ones to aggregate into an hour
      objStat.windows.day.push(
        aggStats[objStat.type](objStat.windows.hour)
      );
      objStat.windows.ts_day = objStat.ls;
    }
  }
  // process current
  objStat.windows.current =
    updateStats[objStat.type](arrData,objStat.windows.current);
  return objStat;
};
```

# Visualizations

> By choosing one dimension, you are actively removing the rest of the dimensions.
>
> —Weidong Yang, CEO at Kineviz (*http://Kineviz.com*)

There are a lot of ways to present any set of data. Many guides prescribe certain visualizations for certain types of data and goals. It can be difficult to know which elements of your data a visualization will highlight until it's been tried. Figure 8-2 illustrates how differently the same set of data can be shown. Some of these look like they can lead to a conclusion or show a trend. If you were to pick only one of these to show, would you be missing out on any big revelations?

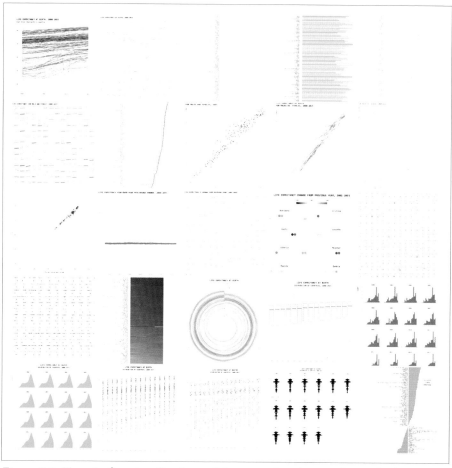

*Figure 8-2. Twenty-five visualizations of the same data (source: http://bit.ly/ 2xp6ene)*

Streaming visualizations are not necessarily the same as real-time visualizations. In practice, the difference can be significant. "Real time" is supposed to mean that it's up-to-date. Real-time visualizations done well keep themselves up-to-date without needing to be refreshed; they show all of the current values. Streaming visualizations give you a sense of the data that is being applied and how it's changing over time. A visualization can be real-time streaming. A streaming visualization does not need to be real-time to be effective. A streaming visualization for a past time frame still has added benefits, such as showing sequence patterns. If a typical static visualization that represents a point in time were updated to be streaming, it would do the following:

- Convey a sense of the data volume
- Show a transition from previous to current values
- Show relevant history
- Allow the analyst to intuitively find patterns in sequences
- Keep as much relevant context as possible with the source data

Figure 8-3 is an example of an interactive visualization that combines multiple elements from various coordinated perspectives. The resulting effect is easier to understand than if only one of the perspectives were chosen.

*Figure 8-3. A streaming visualization with movement, sequences, and statistical context (source: http://bit.ly/2L8lNla)*

# Streaming Options for Common Visualizations

In this section, we'll look at some examples of how common visualizations can be adapted to display streaming data. The following chart type examples and more can be found in the Data Visualisation Catalogue (*http://www.datavizcata logue.com/*). It's not recommended that all of the options listed for each chart type be applied at once. Many of them conflict with each other or are redundant. Choose the options that work well for your visual language to be consistent and bring the most intuitive understanding. If techniques are coordinated across charts, the impact is greater and easier to learn. Any options you choose not to use to represent time can then be used for other aspects (either categorical or quantitative). Be careful not too make too many things dynamic; some stable reference points are needed for quick understanding.

*Dot map*

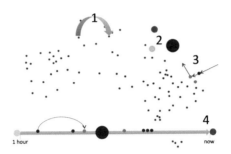

- Show source-to-destination movement.
- Use color, size, or transparency to represent age.
- Add vector arrows to indicate past or upcoming movement.
- Add a coordinated timeline.

*Parallel coordinates plot*

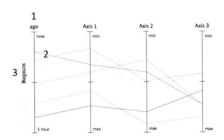

- Represent age with its own scale.
- Distinguish age in lines with color, transparency, or style.
- Optionally allow the timeline to scroll and drop values as they fall outside the window.

*Network diagram*

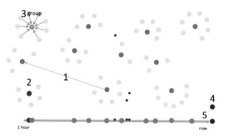

- Distinguish age in relationships.
- Distinguish age in nodes.
- Allow grouping with age.
- Distinguish new nodes.
- Add a coordinated timeline.

*Stacked horizontal bar chart, distribution*

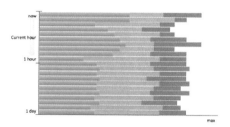

- Create layers for time windows where older ones disappear eventually.

*Line graph*

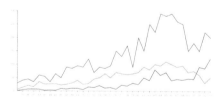

- This is already commonly used as a streaming graph. Its biggest drawback is lack of dimensionality.

*Scatterplot*

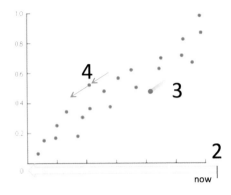

- Represent age of data points with size, color, style, or transparency.
- Use an axis for time and allow it to move.
- Show fading trails for where data points have been.
- Add vector arrows to show recent or expected movement.

*Pictogram chart*

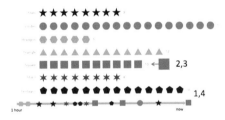

- Rearrange the icons into other configurations, such as order of occurrence.
- Style the icons to represent age.
- New icons enter from one direction and aged-out ones exit the opposite end.
- Add a timeline that is aligned or coordinated.

*Radar chart*

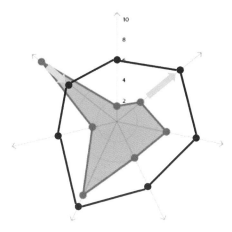

- Represent age with heatmap colors.
- Show outlines of past or future shapes.
- Add vector arrows showing direction of change.

*Treemap*

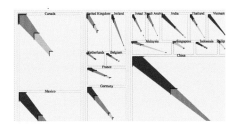

*Source: Elijah Meeks, https://bit.ly/2r9s4V5*

- Show previous positions as trails.
- Style previous positions according to age.

# Streaming Visualization Techniques

The techniques described here and in the previous list can be applied and combined to add new dimensions to existing visualizations. The patterned movement will make it intuitive for the viewer to understand the streaming visualization and help ensure that a snapshot of that visualization will still make sense as a moment in time. The following are some of the options you have for enhancing your streaming visualizations:

- Styling to represent age (color, opacity, line styles, etc.)
- Movement from previous to new values
- Layout and position for time
- Fading trails
- Vector arrows
- Coordinated timelines
- Scrolling time windows
- Time window layers/small multiples
- Sedimentation
- 3D time depth

*Styling to represent age* is one of the easiest adjustments to make to an existing chart. Anything you can do to distinguish the look of a data marker with respect to its age and adjust it over time will add a new dimension. The more consistently you use the same styling across charts for the same time frames, the more benefit there will be from it. You can then do a visual correlation between charts. Styling options include but are not limited to color, opacity/transparency, thickness and style of lines, shape, border styles, and decorations such as flags, icons, or tags.

Animating movement from an old to a new value makes the most sense when the chart relies heavily on a layout element in more than one direction. A bar chart has only one meaningful dimension, which is where the end of the bars line up on the numerical axis, but you can still animate bars—it will be eye catching, and viewers will immediately notice the direction of change. It's much better than just snapping to a new value. The more dimensions a chart has, the more benefit there is in showing movement between values. Scatterplot values that change can be hard to track without showing them move.

Using layout and position to indicate time is a common technique for some charts, but rarely thought of in others where it may still be of benefit. A timeline or a line chart will have an axis dedicated to time, allowing viewers to understand the age, frequency, and relative age of data points at a glance. For other chart types, such as a relationship diagram, the layout doesn't usually help. In a streaming application, new values will usually simply appear next to what they are related to. Displaying them first in a queue area associated with new values and then moving to their destinations helps viewers see how many new things are occurring at once. It gives a sense of what's new, and you can see what order the items are queued in. This helps bring attention to new items that it might be easy to overlook if they just blinked into existence. This technique can be applied to a map that doesn't have a source for the markers to move from.

*Fading trails* work well with moving values. As values move, they leave trails that end in full transparency. The more opaque, the more recent the position. This helps viewers understand where values came from at a glance without seeing them move. The gradual transparency allows trails to not overlap each other and create unnecessary clutter. One of the great things about this technique is that it can show some history of values with a snapshot.

*Vector arrows* are commonly used to represent forces in complex 3D charts (see Figure 8-4). Their length can indicate power, and the direction is self-explanatory. If we adapt this technique for other chart types, it can show previous and predicted directions. The arrows themselves can be styled to represent a number of categorical and quantitative dimensions.

*Figure 8-4. Vector arrows applied in a 3D visualization example of the MathBox library (source: https://gitgud.io/unconed/mathbox)*

*Coordinated timelines* can be added to charts of many types that don't have any sort of time element already. The most intuitive coordination of a timeline is by aligning age with the time axis of the timeline. If the timeline moves from oldest on the left to newest on the right, then it can act like a coordinated frequency and volume summary for the same axis on a related chart. Another way to coordinate a timeline is to place distinguishable data markers from the main chart on it. This can allow viewers to see the timing and frequency patterns of these markers, even if they appear in the primary layout without any reference to time.

*Scrolling time windows* are a variation on time-based layout where the entire chart scrolls constantly. What it shows at any given time is a moving window of time and values for that period. A common example is a streaming line chart, but this approach can be used with any chart that has a time-based layout. When a time-based layout doesn't make sense, a coordinated scrolling timeline can be added to bring that dimension.

Using *small multiples* is a common technique to compare various values. It's a brute-force method for adding a dimension. You can use it to compare categorical variables for the same time frame, or to show values for the same variable in different time windows, as in Figure 8-5. The small multiples technique can be used in a lot of ways. When you have charts that are primarily streaming interactive, moving/living things, you can use small multiples to show a series of static snapshots when that data has to be archived in a report or printed.

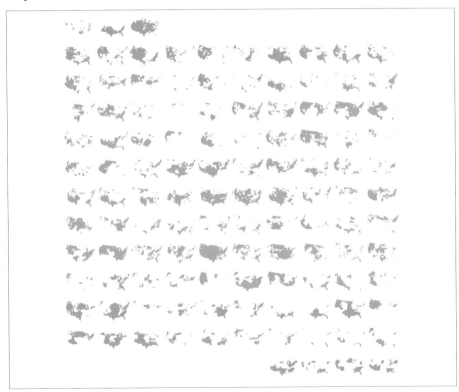

*Figure 8-5. Small multiples chart of drought through the years by the New York Times (source: https://nyti.ms/2LKcCs1)*

*Sedimentation* is a simple and effective visual technique for streaming data. It has eye-catching movement showing incremental values adding to a cumulative whole, but the uniquely great part is that it keeps moving as it settles. The particles that gather can be of varying distinguishing styles to add more dimensions. As long as they have something like color in common and a gathering point, it won't be confusing. Screenshots can be taken to capture data from a particular point in time.

Figure 8-6 is from a demo of a sedimentation component written in D3. It has a few modes shown here that all show how data is added over time.

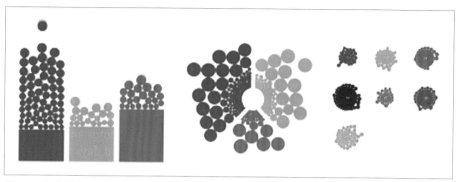

*Figure 8-6. Examples from the Visual Sedimentation library (http://bit.ly/2L9yRqv) for D3.js*

*Depth* can be used as an indication of time in a 3D visualization. 3D visualizations work well with streaming data because the movement allows you to see different values for moments of time before they start fading into the distance. New data appears in front of you and then fades further into the background with age. This wouldn't work with a static visualization or a snapshot because only the top layer or layers would be visible.

# Bar Chart Example

A *bar chart* is one of the simplest ways to present data. It's also one of the most common ways to show data over a time frame or streaming data. When it's used for streaming data, there are two common approaches:

- Show a bar chart per time increment. Use one for days, one for hours, etc. This approach is good in that it shows the context of older time frames while the more recent data scrolls by. The problem is that it requires a lot space and requires the analyst to understand several charts in relation to each other.

- Have one chart and keep it up-to-date by polling. This approach will always fall short in a streaming scenario. The most recent values will get lost in the latest aggregate. If you are measuring per hour, you will know only how close your current hour is to the previous ones; you'll be constantly looking at the time and wondering if this amount is normal for this part of the hour, and any patterns that occur in bursts will be lost.

You can create a hybrid of these approaches that will keep the context of the history at various time increments while showing the most recent data prominently, as in Figure 8-7.

*Figure 8-7. Streaming bar chart with multiple time increments*

This chart allots 50% of the width to show the most recent 60 seconds. These are the most recent values and appear the brightest. Because there are bars for minutes next to this section, there isn't a lot of benefit to showing more than 60 seconds at a time. The same logic applies to the last 60 minutes and 24 hours. The key is for them to be normalized. The minutes, hours, and days need to represent statistics per second for comparison to seconds. Other common charting components can be added to compare things like minimum and maximum values in the same chart. At an implementation level, this can be done by putting several charts inline.

The code to produce the bar chart in Figure 8-7 is shown in Examples 8-3 and 8-4. Full working mockup code can be found in the book's GitHub repository (*http://bit.ly/2sqEgl4*).

*Example 8-3. Streaming data population for multiple-time-increment horizontal bar chart*

```
// init the arrays
var arrDays=[], arrHours=[], arrMinutes=[], arrSeconds=[];
var iSeconds=0,iMinutes=0,iHours=0,iDays=0;

// small utility function to get the sum for an array
var fnSum=function(arrIn){
  var intSum=0;
  for(var i=0;i<arrIn.length;i++){ intSum+=arrIn[i]; }
  return intSum;
};

var fnOnMessage=function(intVal){
  // assuming 1 value and function call per second
  arrSeconds.push(intVal);
  if(iSeconds>59){
    // add minute
    var intSum=fnSum(arrSeconds);
    arrMinutes.push(intSum/60);
    iSeconds=0;
    if(iMinutes>59){
      // add hour
      var intSum=fnSum(arrSeconds);
```

```
        arrHours.push(intSum/3600);
        iMinutes=0;
        if(iHours>23){
          // add day
          var intSum=fnSum(arrSeconds);
          // divide by number of seconds to normalize to average/second
          arrDays.push(intSum/86400);
          iHours=0;
        }
        iHours++;
      }
      iMinutes++;
    }
    iSeconds++;
}
```

*Example 8-4. Angular HTML to display multiple inline simple charts*

```html
<div layout="row" layout-align="begin">
<div layout="column"  layout-align="end" flex="10">
    <div layout="row" layout-align="begin end" flex>
      <div ng-repeat="intVal in arrDays"
        class="bar color4"
        ng-style="{'height':intVal+'px'}" title="{{intVal}}" flex>
      </div>
    </div>
    <div> Days </div>
</div>
<div layout="column" layout-align="end" flex="15">
    <div layout="row" layout-align="begin end" flex>
      <div ng-repeat="intVal in arrHours"
        class="bar color3"
        ng-style="{'height':intVal+'px'}"
        title="{{intVal}}" flex>
      </div>
    </div>
    <div> Hours </div>
</div>
<div layout="column" layout-align="end" flex="25">
    <div layout="row" layout-align="begin end" flex>
      <div ng-repeat="intVal in arrMinutes"
        class="bar color2"
        ng-style="{'height':intVal+'px'}"
        title="{{intVal}}" flex>
      </div>
    </div>
    <div> Minutes </div>
</div>
<div layout="column" layout-align="end" flex="60">
    <div layout="row" layout-align="begin end" flex>
      <div ng-repeat="intVal in arrSeconds"
        class="bar color1"
        ng-style="{'height':intVal+'px'}"
```

```
          title="{{intVal}}" flex>
      </div>
    </div>
    <div> Seconds </div>
  </div>
</div>
```

# Static Information

There are a lot of moving dynamic components in a streaming visualization, by nature. Static reference points or guides can help provide cognitive anchors in a chaotic visualization. The following are some categories of static information to consider:

*Guides*
These include labels and legends, things to help you decipher the visualization.

*Distinct identifiers*
These are the terms that you will use to describe the visualization to others; for example, "the east web server error log monitor."

*Layout*
Having a meaningful layout is one of the best ways to build an intuitive understanding for rapidly changing visualizations. If you know that items in the center are different from those at the top right, or that something went from Texas to Alaska, it helps a lot.

*Navigation*
You don't want to have to chase your controls; it should be easy to navigate between them.

*Thresholds*
Data ranges and thresholds can help you interpret the data you are seeing as being normal, outside of a tolerance, beyond a service agreement and more. They include anything that can help you put the existing information into a context to draw conclusions.

Whatever the visualization is, see if it can be updated to have a sense of movement and history. Even something as simple as a progress bar can have a time element added to it, so the viewer can see how much progress was made over what period. A static current state doesn't convey nearly as much useful information about a dynamic system.

# CHAPTER 9

# Streaming Analysis

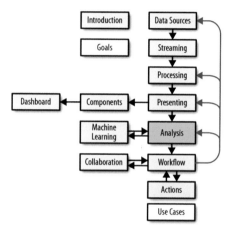

*Visual analysis* is something we do intuitively when we see things. There are particular cognitive processes that we target when we are considering visual analysis for a data visualization. The goal is to leverage the natural capabilities of the analyst while bringing certain aspects into conscious recognition. Here we will go over some basic concepts of analysis to consider when developing a visualization. We'll start with some pitfalls to look out for and avoid, both as a visualization designer and as an analyst.

## Visual Distractions

In the conscious act of visual analysis, we need to avoid distracting artifacts that we know are unintentional or not mapped to any meaning. These are common. We want to avoid them when creating data visualizations as much as possible and try to ignore them when analyzing data through a visualization. Such artifacts include the following:

- Minor alignment or line-connection issues
- Features you don't know the name of or can't describe to others
- Overlapping labels due to the volume of data
- Everything considered to be chartjunk (*https://en.wikipedia.org/wiki/Chart junk*) including shadows, unnecessary lines, meaningless background images, gradients, and anything else that is added unnecessarily

# Visual Deception

A number of things may be done intentionally to mislead the viewer, typically in a sales context where the author of the visualization is trying to persuade the audience. As an analyst, it's good to be aware of these techniques and immediately call into question the intentions of and the data behind a visualization. Equally, when creating a visualization, it's important to avoid the temptation to use such techniques, even if your intentions are not malicious.

There are a lot of fun examples to be found and excited comments to accompany them. When looking critically at any data visualization, if you are simply aware of these techniques, you are less likely to be fooled by them. Tricks that may be used include these:

- Selectively showing a portion of a chart without showing the whole
- Exaggerating or minimizing difference by manipulating the vertical scale (see Figure 9-1)
- Using a nonlinear axis/scale without labeling it as such
- Showing distributions that don't sum to 100%
- Showing change without showing a baseline context
- Plotting data from two different series of data on two different sets of axes on the same chart without establishing their correlation
- The suspicious absence of significant data
- Showing data as percentages without any mention of the values
- Using a title intended to lead the viewer to make a conclusion without studying the data in any detail

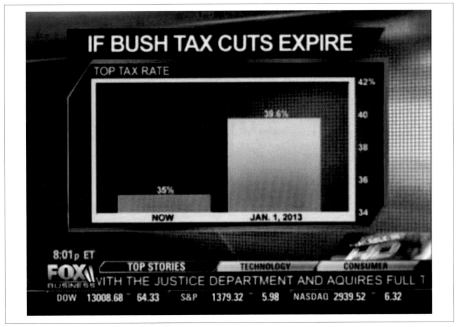

*Figure 9-1. An example of zooming in to a section of a chart that exaggerates a difference by removing the context of scale (source: http://bit.ly/2J50Erd)*

## Cognitive Bias

A *cognitive bias* is a tendency to think in a certain direction—sometimes one that is misleading. The most common bias to avoid when analyzing anything critically is confirmation bias, where you subconsciously look for support for an already assumed conclusion. Cognitive bias is an interesting area of study that is largely beyond the scope of this text (Figure 9-2 gives an idea of the complexity and the types of bias that exist). To limit the potential effects of bias in visual analysis, a few things are worth keeping in mind:

- The visualization shown may not be the best view to represent the context or area of inquiry.
- Don't assume the meaning of colors or other elements unless they are stated or part of a coordinated and consistent visual language.
- The scope of data shown may not be large enough for meaningful analysis.
- The data may have been transformed, filtered, sampled, or in some other way reduced.

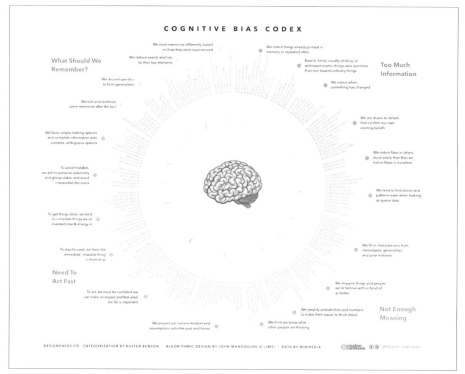

*Figure 9-2. Map of cognitive bias (source: https://en.wikipedia.org/wiki/ List_of_cognitive_biases)*

# Analysis Models

*Analysis models* are templates to aid in the analyzing of data within a specific context and for a specific goal (see Figure 9-3 for an example). They help analysts to see what's missing before coming to a conclusion. These models should be a strong influence on a custom data visualization that has the same goals as the analysis model. They tell you exactly what the analyst is looking for.

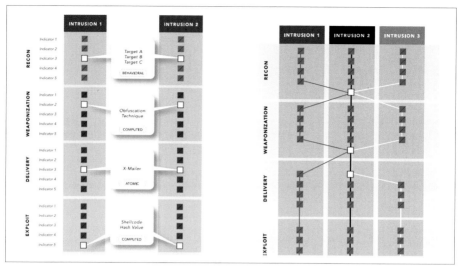

*Figure 9-3. Kill chain analysis model by Lockheed Martin (source: https://lmt.co/
2I1tHfH)*

If you aren't aware of an analysis model that shares the goal of your visualization,
you can create your own. Here are a few key aspects to keep in mind:

*Process*
> There is a specific flow to what's being examined, with several steps. Those
> steps should be accounted for.

*Affordance*
> The existence of one data point should be accompanied by certain others.
> Their absence should create questions.

*Dichotomy*
> Each dimension has an opposite: attackers versus defenders, maximums ver-
> sus minimums, common versus unusual.

You can use these generic guidelines to create a general model that analysts can
then tune for themselves. Layouts or nodes can be created that represent different
stages of a process. Their accompanying filtered data can be shown in each one
and flow to the next. This will immediately reveal any imbalance in a process.
Any relationships that should be assumed to be present can be shown and popu-
lated when they exist, with their absence triggering a style that will stand out to
the analyst. Opposites of several typical values can be automatically added to achieve a sense of scale and balance.

Figure 9-4 is an example of an analysis model baked into a visualization. When
the model is part of the visualization it's harder to break way from it than if it's
only a suggested process.

*Figure 9-4. ProtectWise (https://www.protectwise.com/platform/) visualizes the kill chain as a radar-like spiral with incoming objects; most of the components are streaming*

# Visual Analysis

*Visual analysis* is one of the goals of streaming data visualization. We are trying to use the analyst as a component to recognize things that are intuitive to them and difficult to determine programmatically. With this in mind, we can design visualizations that present the analyst with enough information to spot these things and interactions that enable them to easily enter their observations. Given the right information, analysts are great at recognizing the following:

- Sequential patterns (what typically comes after what)
- Frequency and changes in it (how often something happens)
- Loops with exceptions
- Outliers (especially deviations that are subtle but significant)
- Patterns that should not be there
- What's missing (data that should be there but is not)
- Intentional and meaningful visual elements

*Sequential patterns* are patterns in order. They can be predicted by understanding the underlying process or identified through recurring observations. Whether the patterns are anticipated or not, recognizing them is helpful. Once a pattern is identified, you can predict what you expect to happen next. The prediction itself may be useful. Any deviation from that prediction should certainly be interesting.

*Frequency* is a pattern of time and volume. It's good to know that something has just occurred. It's better to know whether it usually occurs at that time. Understanding the frequency will allow you to predict when something should occur and make its absence obvious. It will also allow you to understand whether a normal event has occurred at an unusual time or an unusual number of times.

Identifying a loop is mostly about knowing the location of the reset point. This is when you can expect a sequential pattern to repeat.

Finding outliers is a necessarily vague task. Programmatically, it can be difficult to define deviations that matter. Given the information with the right visual perspective, people are much better at this. Getting the information is pretty straightforward. Presenting it in the right perspective takes time and experimentation within the context of the data and goals. At first, showing as many perspectives at once is a good brute-force way to approach it. Some of them will show outliers that the analyst will notice immediately and determine if they are significant. These results may yield more definable rules that can be translated into visual cues.

It's also important to consider what patterns should not exist. Not all patterns are good—in a lot of scenarios, problems are regular enough to be patterns. An analyst needs to evaluate each pattern, not just note deviations from them.

What is missing is the toughest and most profound question for an analyst to answer given what they are presented. They have to work with what's given until something better is available, but the question still needs to be asked. Once something has been identified as missing, you might be able to do something about it. You can try to fill in the data if it's available, or the missing data might point to an actionable problem. Alternatively, you might simply note its absence as something acknowledged but OK.

Analyzing the visual elements critically is key when looking at a visualization. It's important to keep the different goals, perspectives, cognitive models, and biases in mind as you do so. A process can be followed to systematically analyze a visualization. The creator of the visualization needs to list in detail all of the visual elements that are mapped to data—every style, color, line width, visual cue position, etc. Then an analyst can look at those one by one and focus on that element. If you just stare at a visualization with a lot going on, especially with movement, you will definitely catch some things, but if you focus on one element at a time, you will miss very little and will understand the visualization better. This will also help you understand what elements might not have meaning attached to them.

# Streaming Analysis Workflow

Analyzing streaming data has some specific added steps due to its fleeting, rapid-fire nature. It helps to start fresh as often as possible. Remove assumptions, abstractions, and filters, and then reapply them as needed. Doing this gives you a chance to see things that have been covered up, have changed, or have slipped through the cracks. Try to get a good overview of the stats, how those are changing over time, and what data is flowing through before deciding on a path to explore.

Your path may start out as simply looking for something that isn't what you are used to seeing all the time. In this case, you'll want to quickly filter out benign key/value combinations. Usually, a number of fields aren't useful and just get in the way of what you are trying to explore at the time. Hide them for now (you can look at them the next time around) so you can see more of the data you need at once. You might need to go through several iterations of collecting stats to get an idea of how frequent something is or in what range it occurs.

When you come across a theory, you'll need to do a number of things to validate it. This investigation will include things such as comparing it within the context of history, similar time frames, and other values. You'll likely need access to some data outside the original streaming source as well. Eventually, you end up with a report that states your findings with some confidence and lays out the actions recommended based on those findings. The entire workflow is summarized in Figure 9-5.

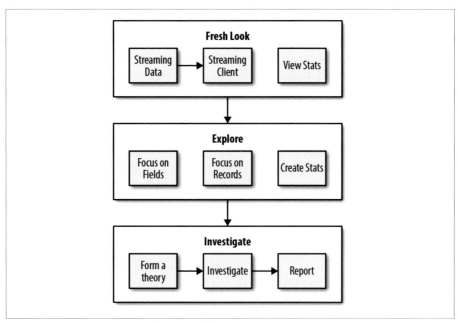

*Figure 9-5. A streaming analysis workflow*

# Context Awareness

*Context* includes everything you need to know that is an important prerequisite to understanding the data. Add any context information to the visualization that is useful. Some context information will be difficult to bring into a display because it's too far out of scope for the data or hard to quantify (what world events are relevant, the rumor you heard from a different department, etc.). One of the best benefits of having a person analyze data is that they bring with them an understanding of many things that aren't machine-readable. They should be able to understand where this data fits in a larger process and what outside events will correlate with it. If you are looking at operational data for your data center and you can't see the major outage that occurred in the time frame being displayed, something is off. The timestamps might be wrong, or there might be too much cleaning of data for presentation, to the point where it's hiding problems.

Here are some examples of context to bring to analyzing your data:

- Where does this data fit in the larger process?
- What is the data supposed to represent?
- What is its scale compared to what's available and significant?
- What is going on outside the data that should be reflected in it?

Knowing where data fits in the larger process can help you know what to expect. If a lot of black-box processing is done before you see the data, it might prompt you to find answers closer to the source. If a lot of data points are downstream of the data presented, you may need to follow things further. As a developer of data visualizations, try to keep context in mind. It's a good rule to try to require as little manual investigation by the analyst as possible.

Next, what is the data supposed to represent? Does it reach that goal or is it missing elements required to accomplish it? Even if there's a lot missing in the larger context, it's important to know what whatever you're analyzing represents so that you can fill in the rest.

Scale is often an issue because of the technical complexity required to represent large amounts of data. As discussed in "Scaling Data Streams" on page 49, a reduction method of some sort will be applied, intentional or otherwise. It's important to know what it is. Once it's identified, you might need to find different angles, see reports on the filtered data, or see the full data in smaller time windows or less data over a longer time frame. Scaling the data to be able to present it is OK, but losing sight of the fact that it's scaled and how is not.

Outside context will always be valuable to analysis. When things stand out in the data being presented, it helps to know if there are any known events that may explain them that can then be verified. It's not usually possible to automate bringing in this sort of information, because it can be difficult to define how different events relate to the data. Once identified, the events should be entered in the system and tagged somehow. Once these events are entered as data, they can be analyzed from a broader perspective.

# Outliers Example

Outliers are a vague but significant factor to use in analysis of data. In order for them to be quickly and easily recognized by an analyst, it helps to automate as much of their detection as possible and then display the outliers in a prominent fashion to the analyst. Let's look at an example: detecting schema outliers.

The *schema* is the structure of the data. If you typically get a field called ip with a matching value in a format like "127.0.0.1," it's good to know if that field gets a new value of "2001:0db8:85a3:0000:0000:8a2e:0370:7334"—this lets you know that something is returning an IPv6 address where you usually get IPv4. It's highly likely that downstream applications receiving this data are designed to handle the data format that existed when it was first developed and will not be able to handle the new data format or detect what it is. One of the first things to check is the fields being sent, as shown in Example 9-1.

*Example 9-1. Detecting unexpected data fields*

```
var objTemplate={ ip:['ip'], md5:['md5'] }
var fnCompareSchema=function(objMsg){
  var arrKeys=Object.keys(objMsg);
  for(var i=0;i<arrKeys.length;i++){
    if(typeof objTemplate[arrKeys[i]] === 'undefined'){
      // this is a new field, do something about it here
    }
  }
};
```

The values can be a little more complex to detect variations in. In order to cover all of the common format possibilities, it helps to use a language called *regular expressions*. There are whole books dedicated to using regular expressions, and mastering the syntax takes practice. A lot of common patterns can be easily found in places like the Regular Expression Library (*http://bit.ly/2IULGYQ*).

I have compiled a few common patterns and given them names in a library that checks to see what patterns match any given value and returns the possibilities as an array (that's what ['ip'] and ['md5'] mean in Example 9-1). The library can be found on GitHub (*http://bit.ly/2IVbZhH*). Example 9-2 shows an example of running values through the data type regex library to see which ones match.

*Example 9-2. Detecting new data type values*

```
var objTemplate={ ip:['ip'], md5:['md5'] }
var arrDataTypes=objDataTester.test(objMsg.ip);
for(var i=0;i<arrDataTypes.length;i++){
  if(objTemplate.ip.indexOf(arrDataTypes[i]) === -1){
    // this data type isn't in the template
    console.log('new data type in msg',arrDataTypes[i]);
  }
}
```

Lastly, you may have few enough distinct values that it's worthwhile to detect a new value. Different techniques make sense at different scales of unique values. The code in Example 9-3 will work for thousands of unique values.

*Example 9-3. Looking for unique values*

```
var arrKnownValues=['127.0.0.1','75.75.75.75','8.8.8.8'];
if(arrKnownValues.indexOf(objMsg.ip) === -1){
  // this value is not in the known array of values
  console.log('new value:',objMsg.ip);
}
```

Don't expect a visualization to make any outliers stand out without some help. Something might be new since yesterday but in all of the data today, and it will look somewhat normal because it's prevalent. It helps to use a visual cue that stands out—like an icon, color, or border. This could be used while showing data or any charts and graphs the data is represented in (see Figure 9-6).

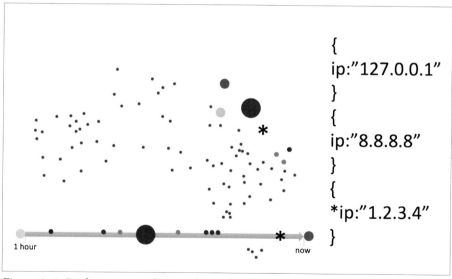

*Figure 9-6. Outlier cues can be coordinated across visualization types*

This chapter on analysis revolves around seeking answers to questions you may not have asked. It takes some discipline, patience, and an open mind to follow data where it leads you, particularly if it points in an unexpected (or undesirable) direction. Visualizing streaming data enables people to conduct open-ended analysis of data more easily.

# CHAPTER 10

# Workflow Visualization

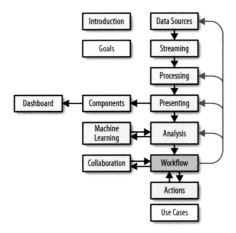

Whether your workflow is a simple linear process that people follow or a complex and dynamic one that evolves, it helps to know what's going on with it. A workflow presentation layer should represent the components in terms that are understood by everyone, showing their status and what activity is occurring (see Figure 10-1 for an example). A streaming version of this would represent the activity between components, using movement, style, and size to draw attention to aspects such as volume, frequency, and latency. All of the same techniques for showing context through time for streaming data can help here, such as adding a coordinated timeline.

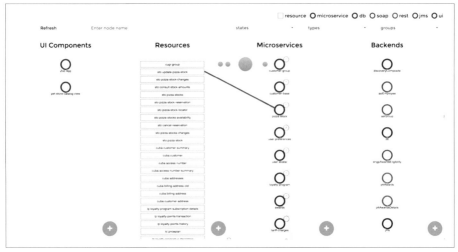

*Figure 10-1. A microservices workflow where things can take different paths to various components (source: https://github.com/ordina-jworks/microservices-dashboard)*

# Updating Processing

One of the immediate side effects of showing the results of data after multiple layers of processing is the observations that lead to a need to adjust the processing logic. If it's something that can be easily defined with logical comparisons, consider allowing an analyst to update the processing directly (Figure 10-2 shows an example of an interface for doing this). This allows the analyst to get the data they need to make intuitive decisions quickly, without having to wait for a development cycle.

*Figure 10-2. An interface for updating data processing interactively (source: http://ohm.ai)*

# Interacting with Visualizations

The more valuable you make a visualization for finding new and significant things, the more analysts will need to interact with it. It's always nicer when we can consolidate tools. No one wants to jump between them and have to figure out how to get data between them. There are a lot of great features you can build in (or put in a roadmap) knowing that they will be useful, without waiting for people to beg for them. For example, you might want to allow the analyst to do the following:

- Zoom and enhance (quickly updating the time frame of the visualization)
- Modify styles and data mappings
- Change the perspective (a complete shift in the visualization)
- Triage the interface (providing fast actions for sifting and organizing)
- Add observations
- Build dashboards
- Change the sort columns and direction

*Zoom and enhance* is reminiscent of the old plot device and writers' joke where the pivotal clue can be found in the reflection in someone's eyeball (or something like that) if you zoom in and enhance the image enough. In data visualization, we often design things to work that way. From a high-level view, you get a broad understanding and pick out things to focus on (see Figure 10-3). When you focus in on them, you can see details you couldn't pick out from the broader view. Then you allow panning to move the view around at that zoom level. This works with a lot of chart types; the more complex and dense the data, the more expanding detail becomes a requirement.

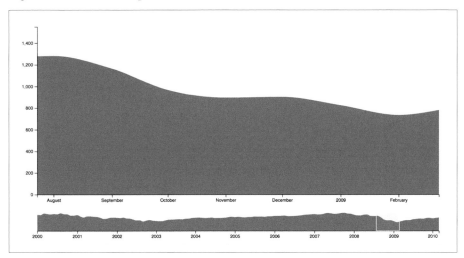

*Figure 10-3. Zooming in on a typical chart (source: https://bit.ly/2lTjfef)*

It can also be useful to allow the analyst to *modify the styles* and what data they're mapped to. A finite number of easy-to-read visual cues can be mapped. Once things are moving with data streaming in and the data density starts getting high, you'll need to be more selective about what things map to what visual elements. Rather than locking in the choices made at a particular point in time, allow them to be editable.

*Changing the perspective* refers to pivoting the data in a way that might make something different stand out. In Figure 8-2, we saw 25 different ways to visualize the same data. Each of those could be considered a perspective. Another way to look at perspective is changing the groupings. You might also shift perspective from data you have to data that is missing. There's no limit to the number of perspectives on data. The subject matter experts for the context of the visualization will need to determine what perspectives are worthwhile to develop. If you are designing the visualization and are not a subject matter expert, you might guide them along by suggesting possible shifts to see how they react.

*Triage* is the most common activity for an analyst, but it's an often missing component of data visualizations that lead to action. Triage allows an analyst to quickly find something and perform a common action on it, such as the following:

- Dismissing data that doesn't belong
- Tagging items so they can be found quickly by those tags later
- Sending records to another group or system

*Adding observations* is a more lengthy action than triage. This might be done in a drill-down view (in a streaming visualization, you're typically drilling down into data plucked out of the stream). Any information the analyst adds can be made available for use in the visualization immediately. Imposing some structure on the observations entered will help in integrating them into the visualization and processing systems, but inevitably some free-form input will be required.

*Analyst-built dashboards* is an eventual ideal. From an engineering standpoint, allowing analysts to create their own dashboards can save a lot of iterations on developing all of the variations that they require. From an analyst's perspective, the more flexibility you give them, the more they can accomplish in the time they have.

## Storing Decisions

It would be a shame if all of that work analysts did in the interactive visualizations was lost. Most of it will need to persist and be used beyond the visualization. It's also itself a valuable source of streaming data to be visualized. This level of flexibility, where the streaming visualizations and interaction with them becomes recursive, encourages creative solutions by analysts. Those solutions can then later be codified into upstream processing decisions.

Store this data in formats and systems as similar to the source data as possible. Reuse all of the same tools. It's important to keep a reference to the data the analyst is acting on when recording the action.

Common and significant decisions to store are as follows:

- Actions
- Categorization
- Scoring
- Verification
- Logical reasoning or explanations for decisions

*Actions* are what the analyst is doing with the information presented. They include some of the other decisions listed here, such as categorization and scoring. Other actions may be things like deleting a record or sending it to another system.

*Categorization* is usually the result of an analyst selecting a value from a listed number of choices for a structured data field. You can have several categories that describe different things about the same record. Imagine you have several analysts looking at the data in a visualization for things to pick out and work with. Several analysts pick the same record and categorize it. You can use this as a double (or more) blind for a period of time to determine things that are in contention or are agreed on. This type of capability of using analyst results is either automated in a system like this or unsustainable to manage.

*Scoring* is similar to categorization, but instead of choosing from a list of options, the analyst is estimating a number in a range. When you store this data, you can then map it, and it aggregates to new visualization elements. Scores are preferable to categories when appropriate because they are so easily translated into statistics, other visualizations, and new elements in existing ones.

Example 10-1 shows how you might store these sorts of data. You'll want to store enough information to clearly identify the action taken, the data acted upon, and the analyst who made the decision. You should also include a timestamp as a record of when the action was taken. The timestamp shown is a common timestamp for JavaScript; it's milliseconds since the epoch.

*Example 10-1. Action, categorization, and scoring data*

```
{
  "actionId": 123456
  "recordId": "unique identifier of data acted on"
  "act": "categorization",
  "cat": "not actionable",
  "score": 5,
```

```
  "time": 1492086375123,
  "analystId": 12
}
```

*Verification* is a type of categorization with a very specific and small set of options centered around verifying data. This can make sense for verifying the original data as well as other actions. The more often an action needs to be performed, the easier you must make it for the person performing it. In this case, verification can usually be as simple as a "true" or "false" (a third state, "unverified," is always implied in the lack of an event verifying). Because it's so simple and frequent a need, providing two buttons for the analyst to quickly use makes sense. Don't forget to reference the data that the verification is for with a unique identifier of some sort.

*Logical reasoning* is the hardest thing to define in a structured format. If an analyst marks something as false in verification, that might send it down a significant path that leads to consequences such as retraining a machine learning algorithm or removing data from devices. If there are a lot of these items that are unaccounted for in any automated processing or algorithms, it would help to know why they are false. The more structured the reason, the easier it is to automate the processing correction and not bother the analyst with it in the future. It's unlikely that all of the possible variables and expressions can be easily defined here unless you provide a flexible workflow diagram builder, at which point it's probably better to allow free text.

Example 10-2 shows how you could store verification data and notes about the analyst's decision.

*Example 10-2. Verification data and notes*

```
{
  "actionId": 123457
  "recordId": "unique identifier of data acted on"
  "act": "verification",
  "verify": false,
  "time": 1492086375123,
  "analystId": 12
  "notes": "It's normal for this to happen on Tuesdays, filter them in the future"
}
```

# CHAPTER 11

# Streaming Data Dashboard

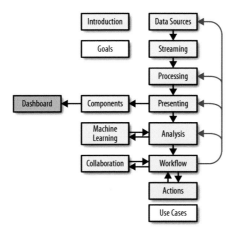

The *dashboard* is where it all comes together. This is the primary point for an analyst to make a decision as to what requires or deserves more attention. The goal of a dashboard should be to give the analyst enough information to make that decision as quickly as possible. A dashboard is supposed to be able to give you a sense of awareness at a glance, but with streaming data it can take a little more time to see the patterns in what's occurring and determine whether the movement and patterns are significant. The more thought you give to where your components are placed and how they are coordinated with each other, the better your outcome will be. Enabling analysts to choose and place any items they want on a dashboard allows greater flexibility, but success may vary, especially with streaming data. With more going on at once, it's more important to be intentional, with everything toward a goal. This may result in you needing to create several dashboards to meet the various needs of your audience.

# Layout

The *layout* is the overall organization of elements in your dashboard. The analyst should be able to get a sense of an item's order, category, and priority of information just by where it appears in in the layout in relation to other items.

*Columns*

Using column containers for organizing content is pretty natural for landscape screen layouts.

The following is an example of columns in Angular:

```
<div layout="row">
  <div flex>column1</div>
  <div flex>column2</div>
</div>
<!-- or if you have an array arrColumns that defines columns -->
<div layout="row">
  <div ng-repeat="objCol in arrColumns" flex> {{objCol}} </div>
</div>
```

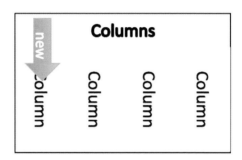

*Rows*

Row containers are well suited to displaying data and visualizations that lend themselves to a wide format.

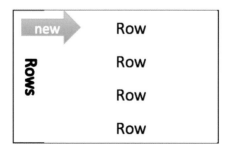

*Hierarchy*

A hierarchy layout has parent and child containers. If every row has child columns and every column has child rows, the relationships are a little easier to read at a glance, and the containers tend to be more square.

The following is a recursive function to create hierarchical containers in JavaScript:

```
/*
Example data structure, with infinite depth
{
   id:'parent id'
,kids:[
     {id:'kid1'}
     ,{id:'kid2',kids:[
       {id:'grandkid'}
     ]}
]
}
*/

var fnCreateLayout=function(objConfig){
// recursive function, calls itself for each child and so do they
self.last_updated=Date.now();
// find the current item
var objElement = document.getElementById(objConfig.id);
// determine layout direction, alternating rows and columns
if( typeof objConfig.layout === 'undefined'){
    if( objElement.clientWidth > objElement.clientHeight )
      { objConfig.layout='dashboard-columns'; }
    if( objElement.clientWidth < objElement.clientHeight )
      { objConfig.layout='dashboard-rows'; }
}
// add a subcontainer for kids
var objKids = document.createElement('div');
objKids.setAttribute('class','dashboard-kids '+objConfig.layout);
objElement.appendChild(objKids);
// add the kids
for(var i=0; i<objConfig.kids.length; i++){
    // add ancestry
    // add element
    var objKid = document.createElement('div');
    objKid.setAttribute('id', objConfig.kids[i].id);
    objKids.appendChild(objKid);
    //if child is missing states, copy them
    if(typeof objConfig.kids[i].states === 'undefined'
      || objConfig.kids[i].states.length === 0){
        objConfig.kids[i].states=objConfig.states;
      }
    // call self for the created kid node
    fnCreateLayout(objConfig.kids[i]);
```

```
    }
    return objElement;
```

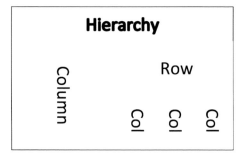

*Masonry*

The Masonry technique makes a compromise between keeping elements in an exact order and filling whitespace. This technique can be useful when items to display are of varying size ratios and the exact order isn't very important. There is a popular jQuery plug-in for masonry layout at *https://masonry.desandro.com/*, and an Angular adaptation of it (used in the following example) at *https://passy.github.io/angular-masonry/*.

The following shows an example of masonry in Angular:

```
<div masonry>
    <div class="masonry-brick" ng-repeat="brick in bricks">
        <img ng-src="{{ brick.src }}" alt="A masonry brick">
    </div>
</div>
```

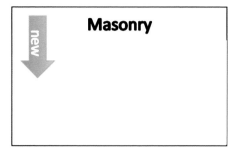

*User-defined*

This is the method of allowing the user to decide the layout of the components (their size and position). This can work well for static layouts, but dynamic ones need something more repeatable. Each "div" window will need to be absolutely positioned with CSS.

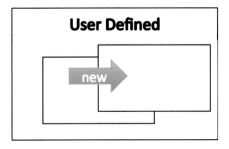

*Radar*

The radar layout assumes the center is most important and that everything radiating out from it is less important the farther out it is. This doesn't work well when trying to display large elements like text records. It's better with icons or something the size of a single character.

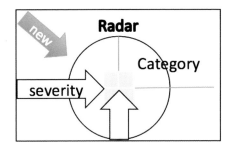

*Quadrants*

Popularized by Gartner, this is a scatterplot with thresholds; each quadrant holds meaning.

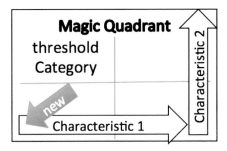

*Hex tiling*

Hexagons are more commonly used in games (*http://www.redblob games.com/grids/hexagons/*) for their balance of flexibility in angles and simplicity. They can be used intuitively and effectively as a layer over a map.

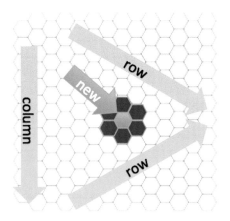

*Experimental*

A lot of attempts have been made at visualizing data in 3D. They have several drawbacks for most visualization goals, but in streaming data visualization for analytics the extra dimension can be used intuitively for time. Anything done with simple geometry like a cube (*https://davidwalsh.name/css-cube*) can be done with CSS and doesn't have to have a canvas.

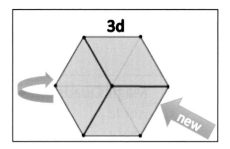

# Flow Direction

Any layout you choose needs to have an intentional and consistent flow direction. After some familiarization, an analyst should be able to know at a glance where the newest and oldest items are. Having an element of priority to draw attention is also helpful. You need the person's eyes to immediately be drawn to the newest high-priority item, and you need them to know where it sits in relation to other items. If the flow is from left to right, with the oldest items on the left as in a typical timeline, you can simply add markers based on priority level. A limited number of flow directions are commonly in use:

*Top down*

Intuitive for streaming interfaces. Items can have a gravity to them. If the opportunity permits, you can allow the items to have sedimentation (see Figure 11-1).

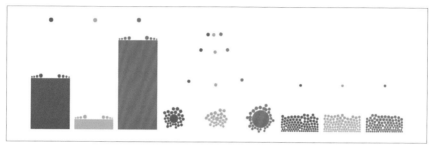

*Figure 11-1. Using the Visual Sedimentation library (http://www.visualsedimen tation.org/) for streaming data visualization*

*Bottom up*

Command-line consoles read from the bottom up. This flow direction can make sense for interfaces that are replacing or emulating command-line consoles for an audience that is used to them. Vertical timelines also have the newest items show up on the bottom (see Figure 11-2).

*Figure 11-2. Bottom-up flow: a vertical timeline (source: https://codepen.io/ paulhbarker/full/apvGdv/) and the lnav log file viewer (http://lnav.org/)*

*Left to right*

Timelines commonly have the newest items on the right (Figure 11-3). When using a timeline coordinated with other things, such as a graph, it helps to have some consistency. You don't want the new items for the graph to enter from the left and the new items on the timeline to be on the right.

The more consistency you have in flow direction across elements, the more opportunities there are for them to intuitively align.

*Figure 11-3. A horizontal timeline (source: https://codepen.io/eltonmesquita/ full/DcHup)*

*Center focus*

A radar is an intuitive interface where new items appear at the edges and their importance is based on their proximity to the center. The example in Figure 11-4 was accomplished with absolute positioning of elements and CSS transitions.

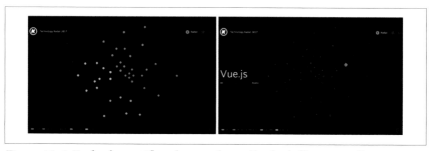

*Figure 11-4. Radar layout/flow (source: https://radar.kollegorna.se/)*

*Front to back*

A front-to-back interface makes sense in a physical environment—examples include a Rolodex or a file folder in a drawer. In a dashboard, this is emulated using something like a carousel or rows of items fading into the distance with age (Figure 11-5). While these can be visually interesting, they definitely add a level of complexity.

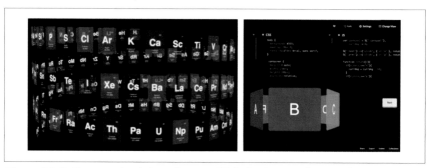

*Figure 11-5. Front-to-back interfaces: a 3D helix (source: https://threejs.org/ examples/css3d_periodictable.html) and a CSS slider (source: https:// codepen.io/nopr/pen/rfBJx)*

# Component Movement

Movement has already been discussed as an element within components. At times it also makes sense to move components within a layout. This movement can be used to achieve a few goals, such as these:

- Showing more information than can be fit onto the screen at once
- Highlighting something, like a significant change
- Sorting containers by some priority
- Showing something new, such as dynamically created components

Some care does need to be taken with too many things moving at once. By their nature, the streaming data visualization components will have movement in them. If they are also moving all the time, the analyst doesn't know where to look, and by the time they figure it out, the component may have moved again. To prevent this issue, don't allow the movement of large components too often. Think about showing a timer of some sort between movements, so it's not too jarring. The movement should help the analyst, not be a hindrance. Try to use movement for things analysts would need to do if it wasn't done for them, like zooming in on something important when it occurs.

Figure 11-6 shows a few example layouts that allow components to by cycled on media that can't show them all at once.

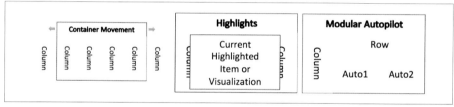

*Figure 11-6. Example cycling visualizations*

At the implementation level, this is pretty easy when using an array to build your containers, as shown in "Layout" on page 126. You can manipulate the array to change the order and what's in it, as shown in Example 11-1.

*Example 11-1. Moving columns by manipulating the array they are built from*

```
// in .js file
var arrColumns=[{ id:1 },{ id:2 },{ id:3 }];
// add a new column to the end
arrColumns.push({id:4});
// remove a column from the beginning
arrColumns.shift();
```

```
<!-- in HTML template -->
<div layout="row">
  <div ng-repeat="objCol in arrColumns">
    column {{objCol.id}}
  </div>
</div>
```

# Autopilot

*Autopilot* can also be thought of as hands-free or demo mode. This is good for something that's displayed on a wall for awareness but not watched intently. The presentation needs to cycle around to display things that haven't been seen for a while just in case. It also needs to have a predictable rotation so that analysts can know when it's worthwhile to look if they are expecting something (Figure 11-7).

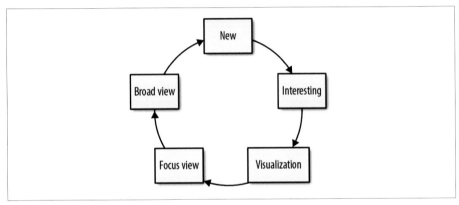

*Figure 11-7. An autopilot cycle*

This feature is easy to add if movement was developed for the dashboard. The logic doesn't need to be complex. The primary purpose of an autopilot mode is to give someone an idea of what they might need to investigate in more detail interactively, most likely from a different display.

The dashboard will be the most debated thing you ever work on. It's difficult to make one that works well for everyone's perspective and interests. Try making one per major perspective, in priority order. Once that's done, most other needs will be met by a mix of the already developed components.

# CHAPTER 12

# Machine Learning

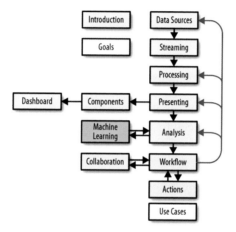

Machine learning is a deep and rapidly developing area. It's become so ubiquitous in technology lately that you'll likely need to work with it in some way in your project. This chapter will provide enough of an understanding on the subject for you to get started.

## Machine Learning Primer

> I believe that at the end of the century the use of words and general educated opinion will have altered so much that one will be able to speak of machines thinking without expecting to be contradicted.
>
> —Alan Turing (1950)

The terms *machine learning*, *artificial intelligence*, and *deep learning* are liberally used and often interchanged. But there are specific times that each is most useful, and they all have distinct definitions. What they have in common is that they are best used when there is a deterministic solution that is not easily defined by processing rules such as those discussed in Chapter 5. To summarize:

*Artificial intelligence (https://en.wikipedia.org/wiki/Artificial_intelligence)*

> Intelligence exhibited by machines. The term has a lot of other uses that we won't explore. This is the term most abused as a substitution for more specific techniques and classifications.

*Machine learning (https://en.wikipedia.org/wiki/Machine_learning)*

> The subfield of computer science that gives computers the ability to learn without being explicitly programmed. This is the most widely used term and set of techniques to represent actual applied processes rather than higher-level concepts. This is where we will focus our efforts, as it has a lot of untapped potential that could be unlocked when paired with streaming data visualizations.

*Deep learning (https://en.wikipedia.org/wiki/Deep_learning)*

> A branch of machine learning based on a set of algorithms that attempt to model high-level abstractions in data. Deep learning makes extensive use of neural networks (*https://en.wikipedia.org/wiki/Artificial_neural_network*). It can be thought of as a brute-force technique in machine learning. It can solve problems that are difficult to solve using other techniques, but is not efficient in doing so.

A simplified way to divide machine learning is by supervised and unsupervised training. *Supervised training* occurs when you provide a known set of examples for each category you need to determine in the future. You then provide a set of features per example. In order to provide the most significant features, you'll need a subject matter expert in the area being categorized. Then you allow the machine learning processes to develop a model to categorize items in the future. It will determine which values of which features are most significant and the weight to give them. You can then test the model out with new uncategorized items to see how it does, and adjust. This may reveal a significant feature you need to include, or that you needed to have more variance in your training set. Visualizing the results at various stages can help with these revelations.

*Unsupervised learning* is very similar, except that the training set isn't categorized. Subject matter experts still need to define the significant features that need to be extracted. The training will then create its own groupings and put items into them based on criteria it determines from the features given. It can then classify future things as being similar to these groupings it has determined. This approach to machine learning is great for exploration and evolution to a supervised training set. It's less practical as an end result because the machine-determined groupings aren't likely to be divided in meaningful ways.

Let's compare the two in the task of categorizing the content of websites. If you took a supervised approach, you would start by creating the categories you need to identify, such as Pornography, Educational, News, Personal, and more. You would then identify all of the features that are likely to represent the key separation between them. You provide all of this information along with any other features that are easily obtained, in case they're helpful in training. You can then take new websites that were not in the training set and test them against the created model to see how it does and identify where it needs improvement. If unsupervised training was applied to the same task, you would end up with automatically generated categories that if you gave them names might be similar to "Websites with more images than text" or "Websites that have a second-grade writing style"—these could be interesting associations, but not directly applicable to the required task.

Figure 12-1 illustrates how known data sorted into categories is used to create a model for sorting unknown data into those categories.

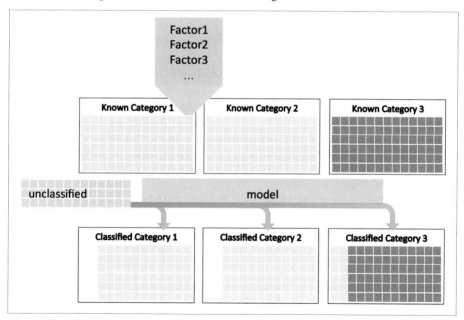

*Figure 12-1. Simplified machine learning workflow*

# Machine Learning and Streaming Data Visualization

Machine learning has been ubiquitous in technology products recently, but presenting the results and using it for presentations has lagged behind. It's a good fit with streaming data visualization, though. Using them together, you can:

- Show machine learning results as data is classified in a streaming workflow
- Allow early insight and feedback from subject matter experts
- Visualize machine learning logic for analyst understanding
- Enable continuous tuning through interactive supervision
- Predict events and compare the predictions to actual data
- Determine what's worth displaying from the stream

# Presenting Machine Learning Results

> Presenting machine learning logic for people to understand is important, but you don't get it for free. It needs to be developed.
>
> —Sven Krasser, chief data scientist at Crowdstrike

Machine learning is being applied in a lot of life-impacting ways. A lack of understanding of the logic will cause a lot of distrust in the results and processes. It's usually not enough to tell someone that you created training sets and extracted features and that gave you the resulting model. In cases where anything must be legally justified, that will lead down a path of presenting the training sets, models, logic, and features and trying to explain it all. This kind of explanation might not be necessary if you develop the machine learning model with transparency in mind.

We employ machine learning when simpler logic-based rules aren't sufficient, but it's still a deterministic problem. Even for things that are not deterministic, it can be helpful to remove some of the constraints and apply machine learning to produce information and options for a later intuitive decision. Naturally, anything that results is going to be more complex than the rules that couldn't solve the problem, but this doesn't mean that it can't be presented and understood. This is when visualizing the logic has the biggest impact. Here is some information to consider providing about the items processed by machine learning:

- The machine learning results, such as scores or classifications (Figure 12-2)
- The machine learning models used
- The features considered and their weight

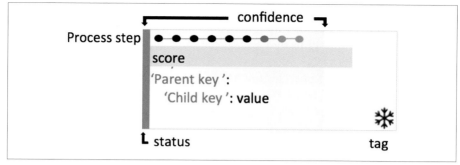

*Figure 12-2. Displaying a machine learning score and confidence*

The score is usually the primary piece of data needed. If you needed to reduce records down to a single data point for data density, it would probably be this score. Then you could drill in for more details. Quickly seeing the score in a way that is easy to interpret is essential to allowing an analyst to make a quick decision. If the score is consistent with the analyst's rapid assessment, they will only glance at it. If it's unexpected in any way, it will stand out from the crowd and can be more closely examined.

The more complex the processes are that are applied, the more important it is to create a way for people to understand what's happening. Figure 12-3 is an example of an interactive visualization of machine learning data clustering. The ability to work with the results gives a crucial level of understanding for improving them.

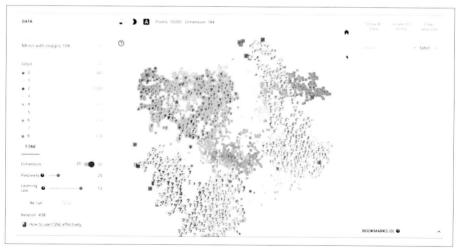

*Figure 12-3. Showing clusters of classified data (source: https://www.tensorflow.org/get_started/embedding_viz)*

Machine learning is being applied to everyday areas of life such as security, insurance, and health. You wouldn't want to be told that your insurance premiums are going up because you will likely have cancer soon and be given no evidence to support this or follow up on. Evidence to back up decisions can also help improve the models and provide context about individual items. When presenting data that is classified by machine learning, showing where it sits in relation to other classifications can provide for much faster comprehension than a text value.

This is a more complex level of displaying processing logic. Figure 12-4 is a great example of how much complexity can be presented quickly to help viewers understand what's going on. These types of graphs can be used in a streaming context in two ways:

- Show a simplified path that represents the individual record's journey through the logic.

- Use the full graph as a template for a streaming presentation of items processed.

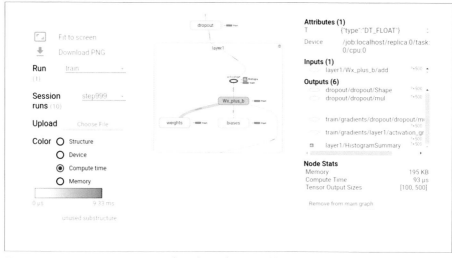

*Figure 12-4. Representing complex algorithms and logic (source: https:// www.tensorflow.org/get_started/graph_viz)*

Individual algorithms can also be visualized. This can be great for understanding an algorithm and how it applies to a small set of data. A complex, automated, visualized decision will not be able to scale to show a lot of streaming data at once. The example in Figure 12-5 shows sequences of characters. This technique is frequently used for all types of natural language processing.

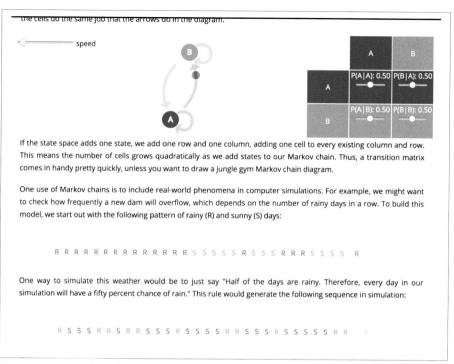

the cells do the same job that the arrows do in the diagram.

If the state space adds one state, we add one row and one column, adding one cell to every existing column and row. This means the number of cells grows quadratically as we add states to our Markov chain. Thus, a transition matrix comes in handy pretty quickly, unless you want to draw a jungle gym Markov chain diagram.

One use of Markov chains is to include real-world phenomena in computer simulations. For example, we might want to check how frequently a new dam will overflow, which depends on the number of rainy days in a row. To build this model, we start out with the following pattern of rainy (R) and sunny (S) days:

R R R R R R R R R R R R S S S S S R S S S R R R S S S S  R

One way to simulate this weather would be to just say "Half of the days are rainy. Therefore, every day in our simulation will have a fifty percent chance of rain." This rule would generate the following sequence in simulation:

R S S S R R S R R S S S R S S S S R R S S S R S S S S S R R   R

*Figure 12-5. Markov chains visualization (source: http://setosa.io/blog/2014/07/26/markov-chains/)*

I've talked to machine learning experts who specifically pointed out that neural networks could not be visualized, by their nature. I found this to be partially true. Figure 12-6 shows a great visualization for understanding neural networks and is well presented. It's also simple compared to what would typically be implemented. At a typical production scale, this type of visualization would be impractical. A production deployment would be thousands of times this size. This doesn't mean a visualization can't be done, though. The goal is to present the information in a way that improves understanding and allows someone to notice issues. This does not necessarily require that it all be accurate and to scale. You can reduce the features to the top-weighted ones, cluster them into types or groups, or allow some drill-down for details. What's important in this approach is that the information is presented in context. If it's abstracted or truncated, that needs to be stated clearly along with where the information sits relatively. If only 7 of 92 features are being shown, that would be an important thing to know, along with how the ones shown were chosen.

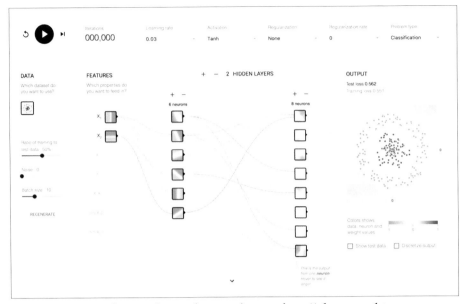

*Figure 12-6. Neural network visualization (source: http://playground.tensor-flow.org/)*

# Supervised Learning and Continuous Tuning

> The longer something runs, the more data you accumulate, and the more accurate you can get. There's a trade-off between gathering more data for training and switching to detecting.
>
> —Sven Krasser

Supervised learning is best as a continuous process. There is a prerequisite critical mass to get started, but after that you need to keep the training sets up-to-date, adding and possibly removing data. Data changes over time, and you don't want your machine learning models to represent only a distant and stagnant past time frame. In order to keep things up-to-date, there needs to be a process that allows a subject matter expert to see some data and the current model's assessment of it. It's not necessary for the data to be streaming, but streaming data has the following benefits:

- Streaming data can be queued but gives the analyst the option to respond quickly.
- There is a sense of time and sequence when the data doesn't come in batches.
- Streaming allows a trickle rather than a flood of data, which can be easier for people to work with.

At several points, analysts can be an integral part of machine learning, including for tasks such as the following:

- Initial classification for training
- Validating samples of what's classified
- Adding information and context to low-confidence classifications
- Correcting false classifications and adding data for tuning

In order for an analyst to be integral in this process, they need a presentation layer that makes it easy for them by breaking down what they need to contribute and providing all the information they need to make a decision. Figure 12-7, found in the book repository under *analystOptions.htm* (*http://bit.ly/2JeHFho*), shows an example of what those options might be. You can create a more granular form, enabling the analyst to explain their reasons for choosing the options.

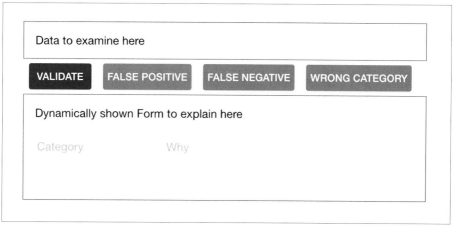

*Figure 12-7. A sample form to allow the analyst to participate in machine learning*

When streaming data from multiple inputs is arriving for an analyst to review, some organization that provides context is required. You can combine a lot of the visualization elements, dashboard components, and layout options we've seen so far in this book to create the set of visualizations and interactions that makes the best use of your analysts in a larger workflow. Figure 12-8 shows an example of queues being used in an analyst dashboard to help them manage the workload.

*Figure 12-8. Queues in an analyst dashboard (source: http://ohm.ai/)*

As analysts work through their queues, the opportunity arises to present streaming data from the interactions of the analysts. Both peers and managers would benefit from seeing what is being intuitively corrected as it's occurring.

Anything analysts come up with that has been validated and can be applied as a logical processing rule can be implemented as soon as processing systems are able to accept the rule change. Anything that requires adjustment to a machine learning model will take a little more consideration to get the desired result. The following common machine learning changes are listed in increasing order of complexity and overhead:

1. Adding or removing a batch of records in a training set. These types of changes can be done easily and need only to be balanced with the time it takes to retrain the model and the number of items required to make a difference of statistical significance.

2. Adjusting the weights or tolerances. This takes some thought, and probably more than one iteration to get the desired result. If the results are used with a wide audience, it's important to understand the impact, not make unnecessary adjustments, and have some consistency. If it's being done on an individual basis, consider retooling so the analyst can make the adjustments, see the impacts, and keep those as their individual settings.

3. Adding a new feature or modifying one. Features and feature changes can be easier to identify than to implement. Once identified, the features need to be created or re-created for all items in the training set.

4. Alterating algorithms used. Different algorithms apply better to different cases, and this is a science in itself. Changing the logic isn't too difficult, but understanding and comparing the impact takes time.

# Presenting the Unexpected

> What you didn't predict happening could be the most interesting.
>
> —Sven Krasser

One of the many possibilities of machine learning and more complex algorithms is to predict an outcome based on past examples. This is an area known as *predictive modeling* (*http://bit.ly/2LKTSZC*). Predictive modeling can give you a range of expected outcomes. You can plot those outcomes with the range of variance ahead of current events and then see how the actual values compare. The ways this takes form can vary as widely as the data itself. You can plot a trajectory of a graph, but it should be a natural and distinct extension of the past data with tolerances, and the relationship between the actual and predicted values should be clear. As with the other machine learning data, you can go much further than presenting the predictions. As data comes in, keeping it within the context of the prediction helps anyone looking at the data make a quick assessment. Providing a way for an analyst to understand what's behind the prediction is also valuable.

If the prediction is based on a pattern of repetition, it helps to see the past pattern, how many factors were included, and how far back it goes. If the data has a projected outcome that is based on a recent trajectory, it helps to see the data and trajectory that it's projected from.

## Machine Learning Decisions on What to Display

Machine learning has a lot of data that can be presented to help understand its results and reasoning. It can also be applied to help determine what to show and how to show it. An overwhelming amount of data that can be presented, but not all of it is equally important to display. In Chapter 5, we discussed some easily defined ways to filter and prioritize data to be seen. Machine learning can be an extension to that. If you categorize a bunch of records that are interesting and can define why they are, you can use that to train a model to give an interest rating to use as a filter. You can then use that score to prioritize records to show and indicate the interest category. Over time, as analysts interact with the data, that interaction can be used to tune the model. Anywhere there is a limit on the number of records you can process, send, store, present, or view, there should be an attempt to intentionally choose which are the most significant. With random sampling, you may choose to display records more arbitrarily, but try to get some variance in the categories that you are sampling to cover as many significant areas as possible while staying pseudorandom.

There are some direct ways that machine learning can be applied to the way data is presented and visualized, such as mapping values to visual elements. Some more interesting techniques also can be applied to much harder problems, such as the infamous hairballs that link relationship diagrams—aka node networks—

when they reach a certain amount of data (see Figure 12-9). At a certain scale, it becomes difficult for an analyst to intuitively pick out patterns from the mess, at which point it's useless. A lot of ideas have arisen about how this can be resolved. Automating the decisions of which technique to use on which links and nodes is a good problem to apply machine learning to. For example, you might use it to determine the following:

- How to group nodes and their links by similarity, age, category, and relevance
- What to cluster and what to visually separate
- What and when to expand and collapse

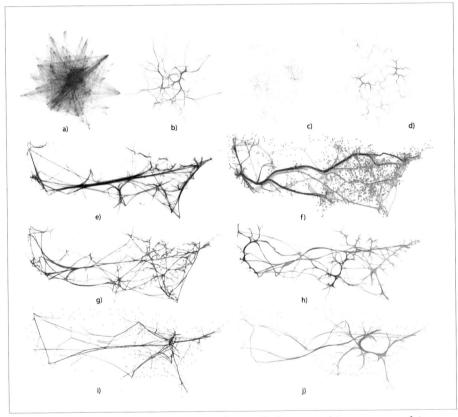

*Figure 12-9. Edge simplification (source https://hal-enac.archives-ouvertes.fr/ hal-01021607/document)*

These techniques are useful in any relationship diagram. When applied to streaming data, they bring extra attention to areas that are moving, such as these:

- Nodes that are added or removed
- Nodes that move or whose attributes change
- Relationships that are formed or broken
- Groups that collapse or expand based on the latest data
- Colors, opacity, or other indicators of time adjusting

This can turn a snapshot of relationships into something that is more alive and in sync with the data. Keep in mind that this isn't just content to display and be interactive with. These techniques can also be helpful in deciding what to display when, and how.

If this topic is interesting to you but seems underrepresented here, I provide a lot of links on the subject in the repository (*https://github.com/SuddenDevelopment/ Visualizing-Streaming-Data*). Many books are dedicated to the subject as well. My best advice is to apply machine learning where it makes the most sense, not because it's a cool thing to do. Use the simplest solution required for each problem.

# CHAPTER 13

# Collaboration

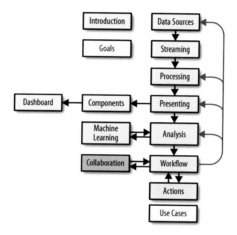

This chapter assumes a scenario where multiple people are watching and interacting with a streaming visualization and it makes sense for them to interact within the system. Anything that reaches this point is pretty successful.

## Why Collaborate

Engaging analysts at a social level brings a lot of benefits. We have a tendency to help each other and work together when given common goals and the right environment. Each person has strengths to leverage and gaps to cover. Collaboration can improve quality and productivity. Here are a few things to support as collaborative features in a streaming data presentation:

- Workflow
- Peer review
- Team awareness
- Team statistics
- Shared perspectives

*Workflow* is the set of processes used to create a desired outcome. Presenting the workflow helps bring an awareness of the overall system. Building workflow components into the visualization allows people to adjust their work efforts based on that awareness, and thus bringing the two together can make a big difference in productivity.

Workflow is relevant to collaboration because it often involves people. Processes may automate as much information collection and processing as possible and even make recommendations for action, but then still present those recommendations to an analyst to approve, reject, or question. The following are parts of the workflow that could be beneficial to display:

- The data required for an analyst to make a decision, including anything that could be automatically added to help them make that decision.
- The queue of things waiting for analyst approval, sorted by priority in some manner.
- The summary of decisions by other analysts, or what is happening to items previously decided on. Was a decision overridden? Was it later determined to be wrong? Analysts need feedback to improve future decisions.

Figure 13-1 shows an example of what a workflow layout might look like.

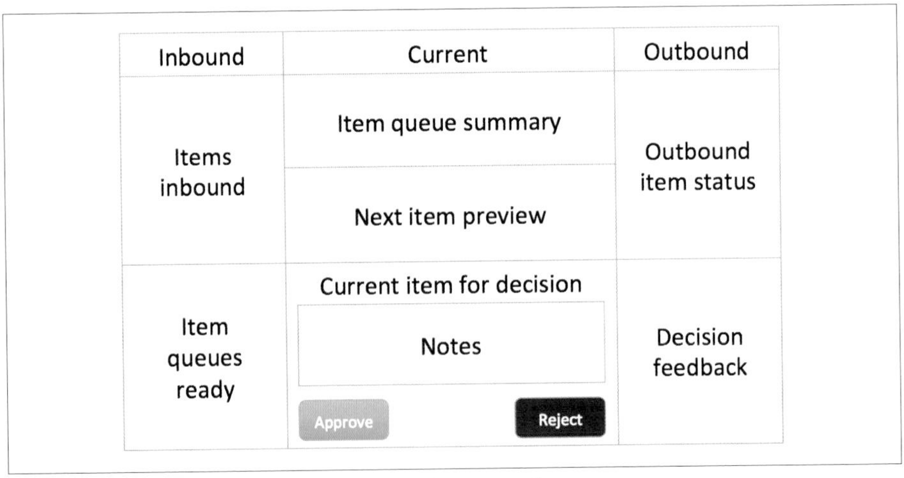

*Figure 13-1. Example workflow layout for an analyst*

Peer review is an often necessary but rarely applied practice. When there are overwhelming amounts of data and everything is time-critical, peer review is applied even less. Creating an easy-to-interpret presentation of decisions and results makes it much easier for peers to review and act on those if necessary. This could be the difference between critical decisions being rushed out without any checks and ensuring that they at least get a cursory glance before they are released to downstream workflows. A layout that supports peer review would look similar to a workflow layout, but would allow viewing of a queue that has already had decisions applied for review.

Team awareness is something we take for granted when team members are all sitting in the same room chatting all day. As teams become more distributed in location and time zones, tools need to be added to keep them connected. Streaming activity into a common dashboard can prompt conversations in the team chat that might not be brought up otherwise.

Team statistics foster awareness by showing the team's activity over time, as opposed to just current activity (see Figure 13-2). This can be helpful for individual team members to understand where they need to fill in, and for team leads to know what might need to change.

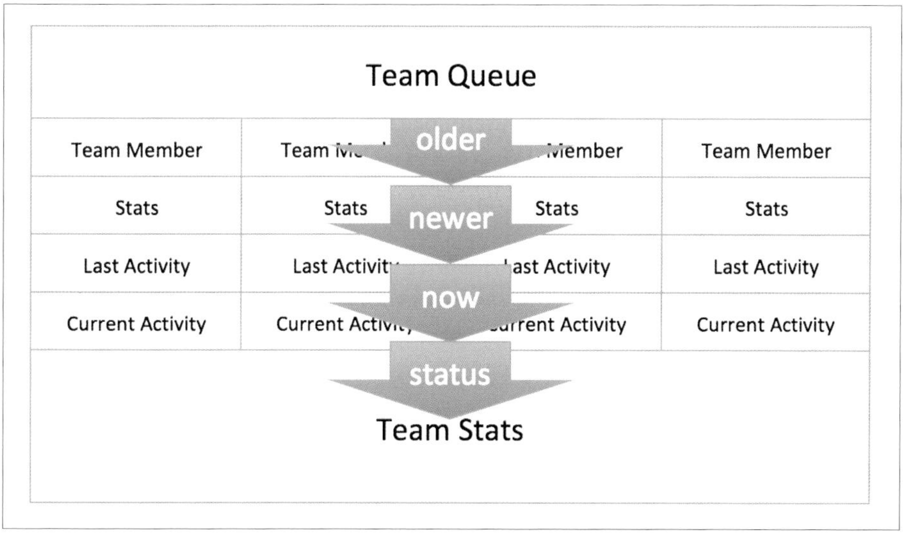

*Figure 13-2. Example team collaboration dashboard layout*

Together, these elements create a shared perspective on the data that is coming in, the activity that is done around it, and the team as a whole. Encouraging collaboration on the data can remove a lot of bias and politics. Aligning a team to the same goals and in the right direction is a lot more than an engineering effort, but creating tools that make it easier is a worthwhile endeavor.

# Sharing Out

When an analyst comes across something that needs immediate attention, they need to be able to quickly and easily send it to an outside system. This can initiate new automated and analyst workflows, or may just be used in an open discussion. The process of sharing outside the visualization system can also be automated. If an analyst chooses a number of filtering, processing, and display criteria that are helpful to others, they can share that as a new stream for other analysts to select and manipulate for themselves. Some outside systems to share data with are as follows:

- Chat clients
- Ticketing systems
- Application APIs
- Another streaming data client

Chat clients are an easy and obvious target for receiving small amounts of data from an interactive streaming data system. It's possible to automate this without an analyst choosing whether to send the data out, but that can make it difficult to keep the volume down to a manageable level. Any type of alerting that is too noisy will appear overwhelming and be ignored entirely. Alerts sent deliberately by an analyst are chosen by more intuitive and context-sensitive criteria and are typically taken more seriously, especially because there is someone behind them to follow up. Chat clients like Slack are API-friendly. You can connect a button and send data to an API, and that data shows up in the team channel you specify (see Example 13-1).

*Example 13-1. Sending a message to the Slack chat client*

```
{
    "access_token": "xoxp-XXXXXXXX-XXXXXXXX-XXXXX",
    "scope": "incoming-webhook",
    "team_name": "Team Installing Your Hook",
    "incoming_webhook": {
        "url": "https://hooks.slack.com/TXXXXX/BXXXXX/XXXXXXXXXX",
        "channel": "#channel-it-will-post-to",
        "channel_id": "C05002EAE",
        "configuration_url": "https://teamname.slack.com/services/BXXXXX"
    }
}
```

Sending output to a *ticketing system* that can take structured data as an import is a useful way of implementing a queue of items to look into and resolve It's also likely that information from multiple pieces of data will be relevant to the same ticket. This will require support for adding to a ticket, not just creating new ones.

*API integrations* for different applications vary greatly What they have in common is that you'll need to map the data from the structure in the interactive data visualization to the API parameters. Most modern applications have API capabilities, and even ones that don't have third-party APIs to bridge them. Allowing for fast and flexible API integrations from your data interface really opens up the possibilities of what your analysts can accomplish. Any return data can also be turned into a streaming data source.

Example 13-2 shows an API call to ThreatCrowd.org using Angular 1.x. Most APIs will have a similar pattern of requiring data for a query. Then the response will need to be handled. This is where you would take the results and add them to information to be presented or processed.

*Example 13-2. API call in Angular 1.x*

```
var objConfig={
  'url':
  "https://www.threatcrowd.org/searchApi/v2/ip/report/?ip="+strIp
};

$http(objConfig).then(
  function fnSuccess(objResponse){
  // do this with what's returned

},
  function fnError(objResponse){}
);
```

Finally, *another instance of the client application* can receive a stream of data after it has been seen and processed. Any number of these clients can be included serially or in parallel in a data stream processing architecture.

Sharing data with outside systems isn't a task to lead with in your project. First develop an application that works from end to end for the target audience. Then revisit this idea later, when it will progress the project toward its goals. Even if this is something you implement at a later stage, however, it makes sense to keep it in mind for when the time is right.

# CHAPTER 14

# Exports

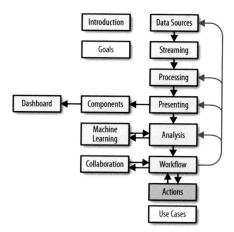

*Exports* are anything that leaves the system for the purpose of importing into another one. Exports of a nonstreaming nature would typically be handled by existing batch processes. Batch processes are configured centrally. If a streaming visualization interface has been created to allow client-side customization of what an analyst can see and what it means, there's an opportunity to use more perspectives with more evolutionary iterations than any centrally developed processes can provide. This chapter focuses on leveraging those varying perspectives enabled by making the streaming data interactive in a client.

When JSON is being exported from JavaScript, it needs to be converted into a string, as demonstrated in Example 14-1. This is required because ways of sending the information are friendly with strings but not objects (for example, URLs or API POST parameters). Many libraries will do this for you, but it's important to note—if it's not done, you could end up with output saying something like "[Object]" and nothing else.

*Example 14-1. Convert a JSON object to a string*

```
// assuming objConfig is the JSON object you want to convert
var strConfig = JSON.stringify(objConfig);

// the reverse process, when required
var objConfig=JSON.parse(strConfig);
```

# Configurations

When every analyst can set their own configuration in a way that drastically changes their view, allowing them to share those configurations makes sense. Once you allow saving and loading configurations, other useful possibilities open up, such as the following:

- Validation
- Different perspectives
- Comparison
- History

Validation of findings requires showing how you found them. If those findings are really significant, including the configuration can also be used to more widely monitor for recurrences. When an analyst identifies something that requires a business decision, exporting the configuration along with the findings is helpful. This gives others the context in which those findings were made.

Perspectives will vary greatly in rich data. Each job function will require different information, ways to look at it, and options for what to do with it. As a whole, the varying perspectives can form a larger picture that is inclusive of the more detailed smaller ones. Allowing analysts with various subject matter expertise to contribute and modify parts of a larger view makes for a scalable and dynamic system.

Comparison between configurations can be useful. One example can be found in network traffic. If you have views from several different data centers side by side, you can quickly determine significant patterns and whether what you're seeing is targeted or nontargeted. What that means will vary greatly depending on the context of the business and networking events. In threat intelligence, a comparison can help you determine whether a single data center is under attack or whether something is scanning or widely targeting a range of hosts. Many other comparisons can be made with other data. As long as JSON is the configuration

format, comparing the data with something like `json-diff` (*http://bit.ly/
2IWJyQr*) should be easy.

Keeping a history of configurations can be useful for change management purposes, especially as these views start to have an impact on the business. You might
need to roll back a configuration or watch several versions for differences. You
can show historical configurations compared to the current configuration by
using a tool like `json-diff` as well.

This sample configuration in Example 14-2 shows a number of properties and
snippets discussed throughout the book. The idea is to have all of the variable
things, such as the sources, transforms, statistics, visualizations, layout, actions,
and more, defined within a JSON structure. This JSON structure can then be
used to run the app.

*Example 14-2. Configuration in JSON*

```
{
  "name": "Configuration Name",
  "description": "description of this configuration that is helpful to others",
  "streamConfig": {
    "addr": "mhn.threatstream.com", "port": 10000,
    "un": "username", "pw": "password",
    "channel": "comma,separated,channels,to,subscribe,to"
  },
  "actions": {
    "email": {},"slack": {}
  },
  "statistics": {
    "hostIP": {
      "type": "uniq", "path": "hostIP",
      "filter": [
        { "path": "hostIP", "op": "ne", "val": null }
      ]
    },
    "userNames": {
      "type": "uniq", "path": "credentials.[].0",
      "filter": [
        { "path": "credentials.[].0", "op": "ne", "val": "root" }
      ]
    }
  },
  "xform": {
    "filters": [
      { "path": "mod", "op": "ne", "val": "syn" },
      { "path": "mod", "op": "ne", "val": "mtu" },
      { "path": "mod", "op": "ne", "val": "uptime"}
    ],
    "decorate": [
      {
        "find": { "path": "findPath", "op": "eq", "val": "findValue" },
```

```
        "do": { "path": "actionPath", "act": "performAction", "val": "" }
      }
    ]
  },
  "visualizations": {
    "graph": {
      "nodes": [
        { "field": "remote_host", "color": "#f00" },
        { "field": "local_host" },
        { "field": "hostIP", "color": "#f00" },
        { "field": "peerIP" }
      ],
      "edges": [
        { "source": "hostIP", "target": "peerIP" },
        { "source": "remote_host", "target": "local_host" }
      ]
    }
  },
  "layout": {
    "cols": [
      {
        "title": "",
        "comps": [
          { "type": "bars", "label": "Top IPs", "stat": "hostIP" },
          { "type": "bars", "label": "Targeted User Names", "stat": "userNames" }
        ]
      }
    ]
  }
}
```

There are some advantages to using the same data format for configurations that you are using for data viewing and processing. For example, it allows you to reuse some tools when modifying and showing configurations as data.

# Datasets

After filtering and processing their data streams, analysts will need to export a series of events as supporting evidence for any conclusions they come to. This is similar to showing the results from a database query. The most natural format for this data is the same format being used for viewing it in the interface, although it may be necessary to convert it to other formats for compatibility. It's also useful to allow showing the data in its original form as well as after any transformations or processing.

Throughout this book, we have been working with records in JSON format. Collections of records are usually going to be in a JSON array. This makes the process of exporting the data pretty straightforward (see Example 14-3).

*Example 14-3. JSON data array export*

```
var arrData=[];

var fnOnMessage=function(objMsg){
  arrData.unshift(objMsg);
}

var fnExportData=function(){
    var a = document.createElement("a");
    var strData=JSON.stringify(arrData);
    var file = new Blob([strData], {type: 'text/plain'});
    a.href = URL.createObjectURL(file);
    a.download = 'export.json';
    a.click();
}
```

This example is simplistic compared to the likely reality. With multiple sources, transforms, queues, and decisions, and everything needing to be buffered and windowed, a lot more than a simply array will be needed. When sending the array of data, sending some context about it too is helpful. If the size of the export is not a concern, you can send multiple arrays and simply highlight one of them as being significant in the data. This should all be reflected in the data that is exported, not a special step in the export.

# Streaming Replay Reports

A dataset combined with a configuration for a streaming interface should allow data replay events. The client can send a series of events that are meaningful in the order that they occurred, possibly abbreviating or omitting events that are not significant but acknowledging that they occurred between the ones shown. The nature of passing on the data like this breaks a few common boundaries. This won't present well in a PDF or on paper. If it needs to be converted to paper to fit existing processes, there are some things you can try that will not be as effective but allow you to move forward. When the events are being replayed, it helps to highlight what the analyst is looking for. Changing the styling of the events that are supposed to stand out so they can be recognized as they flow by can be helpful. If you slow down the time frame in order to make it easier to see specific events, be sure to point out the speed adjustment so it's not misrepresenting the time scale.

Try to incorporate all of the goals and tactics discussed so far into this streaming report in order to help viewers understand the context. Elements you might want to include are as follows:

- Overall statistics

- Specific statistics to make the current point

- Event frequency information

- As much categorical and ordinal decoration as is useful

- Focused raw data where relevant

- Comparison to previous time frames

The streaming data replay report can be so much more than a video of a time frame observed. If the information is curated with a purpose, it will quickly convey a lot more meaning to people who aren't familiar with the interface.

# Static Reports

Downshifting from a streaming data presentation to a static one can be difficult without some tools in place that have been built to help. A streaming replay report won't display well in a PDF or on paper, but a few approaches can be used to convey the essence of the order, frequency, and patterns. These are not mutually exclusive options and can be used in combinations that suit your needs. You may want to do the following:

- Create a simplified, data-dense frequency chart that shows all of the categorically distinct events at once so that the events that are being highlighted can be seen in that larger context.

- Grab screenshots of the streaming reports at significant time frames.

- Show each significant comparison in a line chart with different time scales and time windows.

Static reports compiled from an interactive streaming presentation that are supposed to tell a story will need to add pages to make up for the lack of movement and ability for the analyst to explore. This has a scalability limit that will require some clever planning for anything that goes beyond a few pages of information. As illustrated in Figure 14-1, you might want to do the following:

- Start with a summary page showing the timeline the report covers.

- Show markers on the timeline for the rest of the data that will be provided.

- Include snapshots of anything that can provide context at the time of the information provided.

- Show any summary data between events, like simple or relevant metrics.

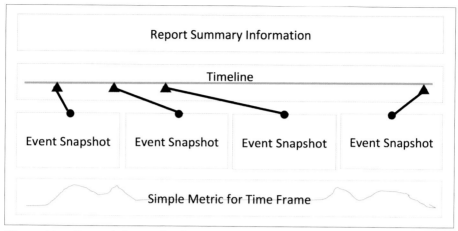

*Figure 14-1. Example layout for first summary page of static report*

# Submitting Processing Updates for the Data Feed

Many of the streaming data sources that will feed into an interface for viewing and analysis will be too much to view in their entirety. Some decisions will have to be made about what it makes sense to show an analyst and what sampling strategy to use. In addition, each analyst will have the ability to transform the data on the client side in order to make it more useful. In both cases, the upstream filtering and processing will at times need to be updated for better outcomes for all.

If data is being filtered before making it to the streaming data client, you may need to provide alternative feeds. One strategy would be to have a feed that is a random sampling and another one that is intentionally filtered by content. The intentionally filtered feed will likely be more useful, but the random sampling feed is important for noticing things that have been filtered out that need to be accounted for in the filtered feed.

Sometimes data processing configuration on the clients is useful for everyone, and it's more efficient to do it centrally. Here are some examples where this might make sense:

- Parsing a URL into its components (protocol, host, path, query string)
- Converting a date into a format commonly used by all systems
- Converting an IP address into a domain name
- Filtering out information that isn't helpful

If you have set up the configurations somewhere that they can be accessed for analysis, you can look for any common processing across analyst configurations and use those as top considerations for central processing.

Exporting is another feature best explored once you have a successful visualization system in place—you need to have something worthy of exporting before it makes sense to put effort into this.

# CHAPTER 15

# Use Cases

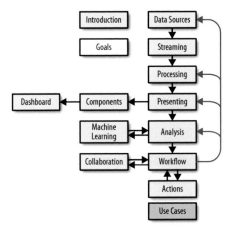

There's no limit to the use cases that are a good fit for visualizing streaming data. Some stand out as ones that immediately make sense and are being used in some capacity today. The common criteria for appropriate use cases are as follows:

- There is value in knowing the recent history, order, and frequency patterns.
- There is a time-critical element.
- An analyst can get more insight by seeing it in motion.

Here we will look at a few examples of use cases that I have run across or found.

# Security

In all areas of security, there's a high value in being timely. The sequence order and frequency of alerts can also have meaning. In computer security in particular, there's an overwhelming amount of data to consume, and new perspectives and methods are always welcome. Visualizations can help us understand the relationships between and timelines of various threats. Security data additionally often requires secondary lookups for history and context that can also be shown in a streaming visualization.

Figure 15-1 is an example of a streaming visualization used in security.

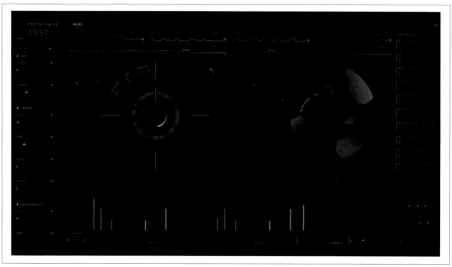

*Figure 15-1. Interactive streaming visualization for security monitoring (source: https://www.protectwise.com/platform.html)*

# Machine Learning Interaction

Artificial intelligence and machine learning are behind a lot of our everyday technology. The decisions made and what goes into them are rarely seen, but the need for transparency increases with the amount we use automated decisions and the power we give them. Interactive streaming data visualizations have a definitive place in providing that transparency. There is way too much data used in various machine–trusted decisions to review it all, but spot-checking should be done (based on definable thresholds and intuition) to build trust in, verify, and improve the results of those processes.

# Smart Devices (aka the Internet of Things)

We are putting embedded computers into a lot of previously inert objects these days and calling them "smart." This is now collectively referred to as the *internet of things*. Each one of these devices is producing a lot of data, and a single modern home can have dozens of them constantly transmitting. Most of them will provide an easy-to-use interface that hides all of the details—the equivalent of the cluster of gauges in your car that tell you only a fraction of the information that the car is tracking.

The manufacturer's display of information from such a device is only one possible view. The data behind it is ripe for custom views, deriving new information by looking at combined data from multiple devices, secondary lookups in a streaming data workflow, interactive outputs, and more. Streaming visualizations are especially useful for presenting information from devices with different manufacturers in a consolidated display, as in Figure 15-2.

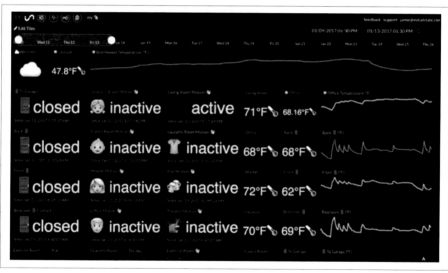

*Figure 15-2. IOT dashboard (source https://www.initialstate.com/)*

# Brand Monitoring

Brands have value. Maintaining them can be intensive and time-sensitive. Streaming visualizations (like the one in Figure 15-3) have been used in this space for a while because social media, a valuable tool for brand monitoring, is one of the more obvious sources of streaming data that needs to be interpreted. This is also a good example of when a streaming visualization needs to be interactive. Basic filters need to be applied to reduce the data volume to something manageable, but what those filters should include can change at a pace faster than the typical development cycle.

*Figure 15-3. Streaming data visualization of a Twitter hashtag (source: https://nuvi.com)*

# Public Opinion

We are in an age of lightning-fast and often brutal memes. There doesn't have to be any truth to them for them to have an impact—the funnier it is, the faster it spreads, and the more it spreads, the more people believe it. Tracking this sort of thing is a good application for streaming data. It requires fast responses by people who can intuitively interpret the images and their intent. Computers are still bad at assessing humor and sarcasm, and things only get worse when text is combined with an image that may have a contradictory subject or message. It's not just what's in the image that counts; it's everything that the viewer associates with this type of image.

If an analyst sees something worth reacting to fast enough, they may be able to stem the distribution or impact of it. At the very least, they may be able to buy a little more precious time to prepare a response.

# Application Data

If your business has a custom-written application, it will have unique information that can indicate its health and activity level. Because your application is specific to your business, this is often the highest place of value to apply custom tools. Any monitoring you have of databases, web servers, and other services will tell you whether they are working at a detailed level, but won't tell you whether the application as a whole is performing its intended function. That's where streaming application data comes in—it can help you spot issues like these:

- Alerts on new sales
- No data from a service that is expected to send something often
- Orders that are piling up but not being processed
- Logins from a new and unexpected location
- Anomalies in the team scoreboard

# Error Monitoring

Errors in applications are common, and there are dozens of applications in a modern ecosystem. Most applications have a log of some kind where errors go. In many cases, getting errors ASAP can save you from a getting a notification that a service is down if you act quickly enough.

An error message will typically provide bare-bones information such as the following:

- Time
- Server
- Process
- Error type
- Details

But it can be useful to give some additional context and an indication of the significance of the error. Consider adding details like the following in your error reporting:

- Supporting service
- Severity
- Impact
- Who to contact
- What to do

It's unlikely that you will know all of these details ahead of time. If you allow the analysts to interact with errors displayed in the client, they can add this information over time. For common errors, that knowledge can then be applied upstream for everyone's benefit.

# Collaboration

The simplest example of streaming data collaboration is a chat client. That doesn't typically require a lot of visualization, but if you were to monitor hundreds of simultaneous conversations, you might need to get creative. For example, it might be useful to visualize the following:

- Channel activity statuses
- Account activity statuses
- Terms used
- Links and attachments

In Chapter 13, we discussed more detailed scenarios of visualizing collaboration and how it helps.

# Workflow

Services often have a complex ecosystem of smaller components behind them. A visualization of these various components showing the data that's passing between them can be a fast and intuitive way to assess the status of the system as a whole. Even when it's usually something just displayed as part of the ambient environment in a network operations center, changes in the typical pattern can quickly be perceived. When such changes are noticed, the analyst will at least need to be able to get enough details to understand and act on what's going on. The Vizceral application by Netflix described later in this chapter is a good example of a tool for this purpose.

# Analyst Input

Data from the analysts is likely to be scattered across systems. They'll typically need to deal with various systems for ticketing, collaboration, and looking at data. A few types of data are very useful to build into a system for an analyst to interact with and gather:

*Categorical data*
    What category something belongs in.

*Scoring data*
    The estimated score for something like severity or impact.

*Contextual information*
    What was going on outside the system that needs to be kept in mind in relation to an event. If there was an outage, a big news event, or a personnel change that is relevant, those could all be helpful details to know about.

Categories and scoring are strictly formatted so that they can be used programmatically, but don't allow the analysts to explain themselves. Sometimes this is necessary. If an analyst rejects something in a peer review, that rejection is almost useless without an explanation. Similarly, if an analyst corrects a machine learning result, they need to specify why in order for the model to be tuned.

# Data Exploration

Sometimes you need to go where the data is leading you. Forget the questions you usually look to answer and take a fresh look. This is necessary to do when connecting to new data. It's also helpful to do it periodically to see if you notice anything new. If you have a mature workflow, it may involve filtering out and normalizing new problems to explore. Here are some ideas of what to look for when exploring data:

*What fields and typical values exist?*

This knowledge will allow you to create a schema or profile and understand when that schema has changed. If a new field pops up or an old one goes away, that could be interesting. Also, if you're expecting to see an email value but are getting numbers instead, that could let you know some data mapping has been changed somewhere upstream.

*Are there patterns that appear over time?*

You may notice that you see a sequence of values that are always in a specific order. By understanding and looking for that, you can notice if/when they don't show up in that order. You can also look for time patterns that represent scheduling.

*What exists that shouldn't?*

Every field and value should make sense in some way to you. Just because something is filled in consistently doesn't mean it makes sense to your business. Especially question anything that doesn't show up in later reports and ask why not.

*What doesn't exist that should?*

The absence of data can be just as significant as the existence of it. If something commonly shows up in downstream reports, and it's supposed to come from the data you are looking at but it's not obvious where, ask how it got there. If an event occurs or you run a test, check to make sure the data you expect shows up as a result.

*How do the values you see impact the system at various points?*

> Understanding the impact of the various values on downstream systems can help you decide what to do with the data and ask the right questions. For example, if a streaming alert system sends hostnames for servers that are used for some sort of automated remediation, you want to make sure the downstream servers can resolve those hostnames.

*Does the data meet the needs?*

> Sometimes data needs to be augmented to be useful. You might also need to capture more data upstream to send along. For example, if something is created without a timestamp, that information may have to be added later and may not match well to the system it's coming from.

*How machine-readable is the data?*

> Anything that you need to work with has to be in a format that is easily used with programming logic. A picture of a receipt is far more difficult to use than a CSV file of a receipt. Free-form notes from an analyst are useful for context but difficult to be used consistently for automated decisions. Giving the analysts categories and predetermined values to choose from will result in values that can be used programmatically.

This is certainly not the end of the data exploration possibilities with streaming data. Visualizing it in different ways can help analysts attain the various perspectives required to help answer these questions faster.

# Examples

In this section we'll discuss some examples of existing streaming data visualizations. A lot more examples can be found via the links in the book's GitHub repository (*http://bit.ly/2kC9rpW*), but these were chosen as a good representation of different elements to discuss.

When evaluating the effectiveness of different implementations, we can use the same considerations that go into building one:

- What are the intended goals, and does it achieve them?
- Does the presentation enable an analyst to make key decisions that are better suited to intuition than an algorithm?
- Does streaming add any value over the display of the data being static?
- Does the visualization give a sense of history for comparison to now?
- How intuitive is it?
- Does it give context of where individual records fit?

- Is it something you are willing to look at for a while?
- Is it interactive?

## Powerboard

The Planet OS Powerboard (Figure 15-4) is a real-time dashboard that lends itself well to screenshotting for inclusion in reports. This may be a benefit and a goal for this dashboard, but reduces its value as a streaming visualization. It's packed with information that is easy to understand at a glance. It shows statistics and detail. There is some sense of history and change. The categorical colors coordinated between the main status area and the details view at the bottom right help relate them to each other. What's missing that might be an improvement is some information regarding the status over time in the main area. The conditions and alarms stand out nicely, but there's no indication of how long a service has been in its current state, if there were any recent problems, or if it has a frequent pattern of being up and down. If a service is bouncing between faulty and available, you either need logic that can recognize and alert you to that, or you need to show this information to the analyst (who can intuitively understand that despite it currently being OK, something there requires attention).

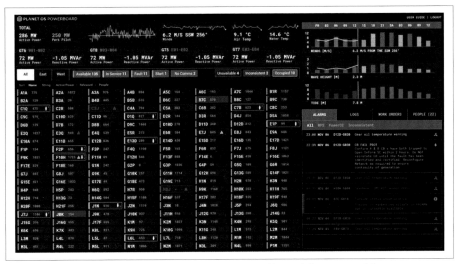

*Figure 15-4. The Powerboard streaming data dashboard for renewable energy companies (source: https://planetos.com/powerboard/)*

## Vizceral

In the middle of moving traffic, [with the] ability to move all traffic between regions, [the] engineer was about to start moving traffic, saw Vizceral running, and said "Oh shit"—the code he wrote would've moved all traffic to one region and brought the whole service down for some and [caused] poor performance for others.

Before this project we had 42 line charts to represent the same information, and it took about 5 minutes to understand what we can get at a glance now.

—Casey Rosenthal, engineering manager at Netflix

Vizceral is a project developed and open sourced by Netflix. As a screenshot, it doesn't make much sense. As a streaming visualization, it's a wonderful example. The screenshot in Figure 15-5 is one of several that would be required to fully explain the tool's capabilities. I encourage you to watch the videos and read the information provided by two of its creators (Casey Rosenthal and Justin Reynolds, who I had the opportunity to talk to while working on this book) in their blog post (*http://techblog.netflix.com/2016/08/vizceral-open-source.html*).

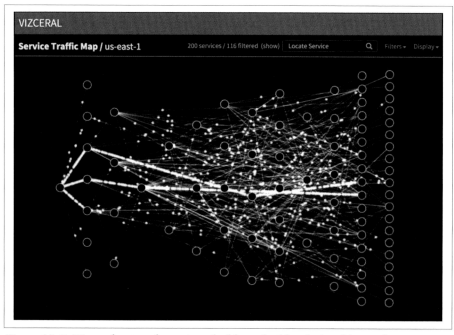

*Figure 15-5. Vizceral network services dashboard with relationships and representative traffic (source: http://techblog.netflix.com/2016/08/vizceral-open-source.html)*

This is a good example of the possibilities when you are not limited to something that presents well in a print copy. It's interactive, allowing the analyst to zoom in and out to different detail levels and move things around to remove clutter around areas of focus. The goal was to give an intuitive understanding of the traffic between services, not necessarily an accurate one. This is an important distinction to make. At the level of traffic that the analyst sees, trying to represent one of anything as a dot in the traffic flow would result in a solid line of dots along all the lines.

Allowing the visualization to be representative and give an impression makes it possible to quickly understand the relative traffic patterns. Because the traffic dots travel in a line, you do get some idea of history. The varying line lengths don't hold any meaning beyond the relationships they represent, though, so comparing any order or history patterns between lines is difficult. One dimension that is missing is any visual indicators of what might be normal; you can quickly understand where the most traffic is and interactively find out what those services are, but you cannot quickly tell whether that's normal and OK or it needs attention. Abstracting the presentation to convey a sense of the traffic can give the necessary impression that is easier to understand the system and the way it's represented in this visualization over time.

## Alooma Live

Alooma Live (Figure 15-6) is the only general-purpose streaming presentation we'll look at here. It does a rare, good job of showing statistics, visualizations, and detail at once in a coordinated fashion. The categorical colors tie all three elements together. When you see something of interest, you can immediately look at the history and stats for it to get an idea of how common it is. The visualization is a simple flow of particles that are color-coordinated to the other aspects. Alone, it might be hard to read, but it's coordinated with a bar chart so that aggregate volumes in small increments can be seen at a glance. Any significant difference in volume would immediately stand out through the difference in movement of the particles. Beyond that, it's hard to rate how this dashboard will fit your goals. It's largely up to the analyst and developer to appropriately assign categories in the data and map them to the elements of the visualization to get the most out of it.

Figure 15-6. Alooma data dashboard for mixed sources, showing the full data, stats, and a streaming visualization of the relative flows (source: https:// www.alooma.com/blog/kafka-realtime-visualization)

# Stream-Viz

Lastly, we come to an example that represents a typical streaming data visualization. Stream-Viz is modular; it shows some current data that refreshes and a few streaming line graphs. It's set up in a column layout where columns can easily be added for a repeat of components mapped to a different focus (Figure 15-7).

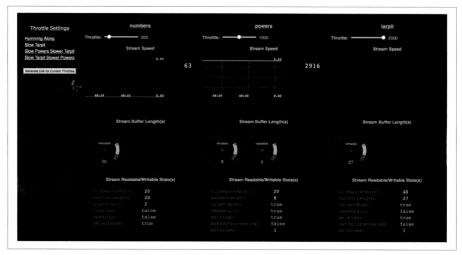

*Figure 15-7. A good representation of a typical streaming visualization (source: http://thlorenz.com/stream-viz/)*

This is a good example of a real-time dashboard that misses the goals of a streaming data visualization. In this respect, it's typical of many so-called streaming data visualizations. It shows current values without showing any real history. It also abstracts away any details about the data behind it. What it does well is remain intuitive; there is nothing overwhelming that requires a learning curve.

Don't be constrained by the examples that are discussed here. All that really matters is that you can imagine some added value to your data if it were streamed as opposed to being static. If a static display is just as helpful, use that. If there's something more to be gained by showing movement, order, and patterns of frequency, consider developing a streaming visualization.

# CHAPTER 16

# Summary and References

Decide what you'd like to achieve. What impact are you looking to have? What in your workflow could benefit from regular human interaction or already involves a lot of human interaction? What benefit could knowing complex information before tomorrow provide? This should help give some basic direction on whether to develop a web, native, or mobile app and what data to look for. So that you aren't overwhelmed with a giant pie in the sky, it might also help to define the time frame and people you have available to work on the project.

## Links Mentioned

The links mentioned throughout this book and links to additional references can be found in the book's GitHub repository (*http://bit.ly/2LE9dLz*).

## Data

You can approach your visualization project from at least three angles to help fill in the blanks:

- What data do you already have that you can stream? If it's being written to a database, you can stream transaction logs. If it's written to a log, you can stream the log updates. Often, listing the data you have available will bring new ideas to mind about what you can do, not just fill in the blanks for your original plan.

- What data do you need to accomplish your goals? Try to think about this without considering current obstacles. There are a lot of ways to get the data you need. The obvious approaches, like getting it from an existing API or database, may not meet your needs. Think about how you could get the data you want; you can decide later if it's worth doing.

- What information requires a secondary lookup? Is that information necessary to make a decision on an event? Data lookups are usually slow and have scalability limits. Try to do them only when the event data justifies it and when the additional information makes the difference in an analyst being able to make a decision.

Now revisit your goals. How realistic are they based on the data that you can identify? You either need to find data that will support your goals or adjust your goals to something your data can support. There isn't much point in proceeding without having worthwhile goals that you know your data can support.

## Transform and Filter

The data you get is usually not in the format an analyst needs to make a decision quickly. It's much easier for the analyst if you transform it inline rather than making them do it. Any data that is completely unnecessary should be hidden—screen real estate is precious. Even if the of records displayed is the same, the less clutter, the better. In addition to transforming data for analysts, you also want to make it easier for them to process logically. An analyst can easily read a comma-separated list of values, but it's hard to do any sort of interactive actions or processing with individual items in that list until it's turned into an array.

Here are some common examples of inline data transformations that are useful:

- Setting timestamps to the same time zone and format. Many systems express time as seconds since a certain time (usually the Unix epoch). That's useful for systems but needs to be translated to be readable.

- Parsing URLs into host, protocol, file path, and query string parameters. Query string parameters are often serialized in unreadable formats, like Base64-encoded strings. Decoding these values is necessary for an analyst to make any decisions about them.

- Translating identifiers into meaningful names. Identifiers are often complex to ensure that they are unique (such as random strings of 32 characters), but these are not useful to an analyst and need to be translated to names that are meaningful.

## Presentation Dashboards and Components

Expect to create a dashboard page for each role in a workflow. If you have a manager, analyst, operator, and automated system, those are at least four dashboards to start with. Each one will also need varying levels of detail to drill down to. From there, break down what each requires to accomplish its mission. You may find a lot of common elements between the dashboards, and you can consolidate and reuse features. Trying from the beginning to make one view work for all roles and levels will be a lot harder to get it right than merging common things that are a good natural fit. For example, both a manager and an analyst will be interested in application logs, but they need to view them from different perspectives. Application events might be the primary queue of tasks to resolve for an analyst and one of many data points for a manager. Figure 16-1 shows an example of how the dashboards for three different roles can share common components.

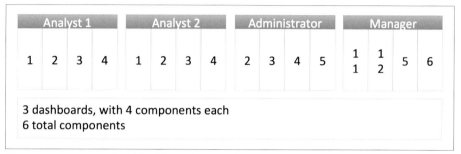

Figure 16-1. Example of dashboards per role with shared components

# Interactions and Actions

How can your different roles be best integrated into a data flow? Assess what they do now and how that might translate to their roles in an integrated team system. Step these actions through the workflow and see what impact they have on the individual records and the queues and groupings they are in. There's a good chance that the system you're developing will allow for additional helpful interactions that weren't possible before. For example, you could automate a double-blind categorization by analysts and randomly pull samples for peer review.

# Beyond the System

You will run into limits in your quest for ever greater interaction and integration between analysts and their data flows. You need to be realistic about those limitations, and plan for various outputs until they are no longer needed. Common scenarios for exporting data are as follows:

- Creating a ticket
- Creating an incident report
- Exporting resulting data
- Exporting analyst configurations
- Sending alerts via chat, email, or phone

# Index

## A

action
  defined, 22
  storing, 123
adjacency (visual element), 73
age, styling to represent, 100
aggregates, 4
alignment (visual element), 71
Alooma Live, 173
analysis, 107-118
  cognitive bias, 109
  models, 110
  of streaming data (see streaming analysis)
  outliers example, 116-118
  pre-batch, 15
  visual analysis, 112
  visual deception, 108
  visual distractions, 107
analyst queue, 16
analysts
  defined, 4
  input from, 168
analytics, visualizations for, 13
AngularJS, 7, 59
AngularJS Material, 59
API integrations, 153
API lookups, 41
API polling, 32
application lookups, 42
applications
  custom-written, 166
  error monitoring, 167
  for data visualization, 6
artificial intelligence, defined, 136
atomic data, 22

augmented reality, 87
autopilot, 134

## B

background (visual element), 69
bar charts, 103
Base64 data, 6
batch processing, 35
  microservices and, 38
  pre-batch analysis, 15
  with JSON Collection Decorator, 44
bias, cognitive, 109
binary data, 6
binlog, 24
border (visual element), 70
brand monitoring, 165
browser-based client, 56
buffering, 32
business intelligence, 2

## C

categorization, storing of, 123
categorized actions, 22
chat clients, 152
client application development, 55-61
  alternative approaches, 61
  code structure, 59-61
  common approach to, 57
  frameworks and libraries, 56
  libraries for sample application, 58
  native vs. browser, 56
  sample application, 57-61
cognitive bias, 109
collaboration, 149-153
  chat client use case, 168

fonts, 71
frameworks, for client application development, 56

## G

goals, 9-20
  analyst queue, 16
  asking new questions, 18
  data pipeline visualization, 17
  pre-batch analysis, 15
  presentation, 10-15
  seeing frequency and order, 19
  showing movement on a map, 18

## H

hardware-bound scaling, 50
hex data, 6
Hex tiling, 130
hierarchy layout, 127
honeypot data, 81
HTML, client development and, 56
http-server, 61

## I

icons, 76
images (visual element), 75
Immutable.js, 79
inline processing, 36
internet of things, 165

## J

JSON Collection Decorator, 44
JSON data, 5, 7
  configuration for export, 156
  converting to string for export, 155
justification (visual element), 71

## K

key/value pairs, 5

## L

layout
  as visual element, 72, 100
  of dashboard, 126-130
libraries, for client application development, 56, 58
log files, tailing, 1, 66
logical reasoning, defined, 124

logs, presentation, 66
lookups, 40

## M

machine learning, 135-147
  basics, 135-137
  decisions on what to display, 145-147
  defined, 136
  interaction use cases, 164
  presenting results, 138-141
  presenting the unexpected, 145
  streaming data visualization, 138
  supervised learning and continuous tuning, 142-144
map, showing movement on, 18
Masonry layout technique, 128
MEAN stack, 7
meme tracking, 166
messages, defined, 22
microservices architecture, processing patterns in, 37-39
Moment.js, 79
MongoDB, 7
movement
  as visual element, 77, 100
  of dashboard components, 133
  showing on map, 18

## N

native client, 56
Netflix
  streaming visualization example, 53
  Vizceral, 171
neural networks, 136, 141
Node.js, 7
normalization of events for processing, 42

## O

operational intelligence, 2
outliers
  in streaming analysis, 116-118
  in visual analysis, 113

## P

Papa Parse library, 31
patterns
  sequential, 112
  that should not exist, 113
peer review, 151

perspective, changing, 122
phishing, 40
Planet OS Powerboard, 171
polling
     API, 32
     updating bar charts with, 103
position (visual element), 74, 100
Powerboard, 171
predictive modeling, 145
presentation of streaming data, 63-87
     aligning with goals, 10-15
     appropriate displays, 85-87
     client application development, 55-61
     context in, 81
     dashboards for, 67, 125-134
          (see also dashboards)
     data density, 78
     events, 65
     logs, 66
     position in processing pipeline, 51-53
     records, 66
     showing streaming data, 64-66
     time references, 78-80
     time to live, 80
     visual elements/properties, 67-74
     visual language, 83
processing, 35
     (see also batch processing)
     checklist for, 45
     extracting value from data, 43
     inline, 36
     JSON Collection Decorator, 44
     lookups, 40
     normalizing events, 42
     patterns, 36-40
     presentation of data in context of, 51-53
     record context checklist, 49
     scaling data streams, 49-51
     streaming data for visualization, 35-53
     streaming statistics, 46-48
     submitting updates for data feed, 161
     updating for workflow visualization, 120
public opinion monitoring, 166
publication, 29
publisher/subscriber channel, 30

## R

raw data visualization, 4
React, 61
real-time visualization, 6

record
     as component of visualizations, 89
     context checklist for data, 49
     defined, 22
     presentation, 66
reference points, static, 106
regular expressions (regex), 116
relational databases, 24
replay reports, exporting, 159
reports, visualization in, 11

## S

sales data visualization, 10
sampling, 49
Scalable Vector Graphics (SVG), 56
scaling
     and context, 115
     data streams, 49-51
schema
     and managing multiple data sources, 24
     defined, 22
     outliers, 116
scoring, defined, 123
scrolling time windows, 101
security
     honeypot data, 81
     use cases, 164
sedimentation, 102
sequential patterns, 112
services, for streaming data, 30
shape (visual element), 76
sharing of data with outside systems, 152-153
     (see also exports)
size (visual element), 70
small multiple charts, 102
smart devices/smartphones
     screen limitations, 85
     use cases, 165
sources of data (see data sources)
spacing (visual element), 73
sparkline, 64
SpringRain streaming network visualization,
     83
standards, visualization, 3
static reports, 160
static visualization, 6
statistics
     as component of visualizations, 90-92
     for streaming data, 46-48
     types of, 47

workflow, 119-124
    collaboration and, 150
    dashboards for roles in, 176
    defined, 150
    interacting with visualizations, 120
    storing decisions, 122-124
    updating processing, 120
    use cases, 168

# X

XML data, 5

# Z

ZongJi library, 31
zoom and enhance, 121

## About the Author

**Anthony Aragues** is currently the VP of security at Bluefin Payment Systems. Prior to Bluefin, Anthony was the vice president of product management at Anomali and led engineering at Norse. He started his career in technology and security in the Marine Corps in 1997 and in 2008, helped build McAfee's Global Threat Intelligence program where he was an inventor of multiple patents on threat intelligence and online identity risk scoring. Anthony has extensive experience in startups as well as large companies—including senior roles in development, architecture, security, and management. In addition, he has been a technology evangelist, presenting regularly at security conferences, including various ISACs. Beyond security and architecture, Anthony's expertise includes front-end user interfaces with an emphasis on real-time visualizations. Anthony has a B.S. in Computer Information Systems from Strayer University, as well as an A.A. in Visual Art.

## Colophon

The animal on the cover of *Visualizing Streaming Data* is the French grunt (*Haemulon flavolineatum*). This saltwater fish is native to the western Atlantic Ocean and Gulf of Mexico, and is typically found schooling among reefs at depths of up to 200 feet. Its its body is striped in yellow and silver, with yellow fins, and it can grow up to one foot in length, though the average grunt is only half as large.

A crepuscular feeder subsisting primarily on krill and other invertebrates, this fish is rarely found outside the reefs and grasses it calls home. The French grunt is a popular fish to house in home and public aquariums, and it is valuable in commercial fishing operations as both food and bait.

Many of the animals on O'Reilly covers are endangered; all of them are important to the world. To learn more about how you can help, go to *animals.oreilly.com*.

The cover image is an illustration by Karen Montgomery, based on a black and white engraving from Georges Cuvier's *Histoire naturelle des poissons*. The cover fonts are URW Typewriter and Guardian Sans. The text font is Adobe Minion Pro; the heading font is Adobe Myriad Condensed; and the code font is Dalton Maag's Ubuntu Mono.

# Learn from experts.
# Find the answers you need.

Sign up for a **10-day free trial** to get **unlimited access** to all of the content on Safari, including Learning Paths, interactive tutorials, and curated playlists that draw from thousands of ebooks and training videos on a wide range of topics, including data, design, DevOps, management, business—and much more.

## Start your free trial at:
## oreilly.com/safari

(No credit card required.)